AF255212

"Two friends have written a book. Their theology of church resurrection is solid theology. Their wisdom is solid trench wisdom. Their love for the church is true love. I commend this to you if you dare to believe that the bones of tired churches can live again."

—**DAN BOONE**, president, Trevecca Nazarene University

"Barrett and Skinner challenge our minds and hearts with this probing question: Can a church experience revitalizing new beginnings while launching new 'centers of holy fire'? We celebrate the new communities of faith *and* the Holy-Spirit-breathed 'new life' for existing churches! Read this inspiring book and embrace the dream!"

—**JERRY D. PORTER**, general superintendent emeritus, Church of the Nazarene

"Finally, someone addressed the elephant in the room! Church planting and revitalization are not competing ideas fighting over the same people and resources. For decades I have heard clergy fret over 'too much focus on planting new churches' and 'not enough on the existing churches!' I believe God has given Barrett and Skinner the vision for the direction of leadership for the church. The question is do we have the courage to follow?"

—**J. FRED HUFF**, director of new church development, Georgia District Church of the Nazarene

Revitalize to Plant

Revitalize to Plant

Reshaping the Established Church to Plant Churches

Desmond Barrett
and **Jeffery D. Skinner**

Foreword by Mark Bane

WIPF & STOCK · Eugene, Oregon

REVITALIZE TO PLANT
Reshaping the Established Church to Plant Churches

Wipf & Stock
An Imprint of Wipf and Stock Publishers
199 W. 8th Ave., Suite 3
Eugene, OR 97401

www.wipfandstock.com

PAPERBACK ISBN: 978-1-6667-5814-6
HARDCOVER ISBN: 978-1-6667-5815-3
EBOOK ISBN: 978-1-6667-5816-0

01/03/23

I am personally grateful to Rev. Darron Farmer who has
shown this revitalizer what true grit, and determination
is all about as he serves in the local church. Darron is
not only a friend, but an established church pastor who
works tirelessly daily to serve his local church. I dedicate
to him the pages within this work as he has inspired
many of the thoughts laid forth in this resource.
D. B.

I would like to dedicate this book to my wife, Dr. Lisa
Skinner, who has been by my side for over thirty years. She
has never hesitated to support me in any endeavor I have
ever had a dream of doing and that includes this one. She
has been by my side in the planting of churches along with
my children Blaine and Hayden. She has never strayed to
the right or to the left but has always been faithful to God.
J. D. K

Contents

Foreword

Anyone who has ever pastored more than one church in their ministry life will be able to identify with this book and its authors. As I read it, my mind went back to the many difficulties challenges and blessings experienced in my now thirty-six years of pastoral ministry. The challenge to revitalizing a church is enhanced by the dream that there is a long term and larger purpose than to simply have a healthy church. The authors acknowledge that ultimate goal of church health is to reproduce new churches. When we see revitalization efforts with this larger purpose it makes one feel like the patriarch of a family that will have a lasting heritage, to reproduce.

It is a great blessing to have leaders in Jesus' church that care as deeply about church health and church planting as the authors of this helpful work do. It is clear from reading that both Jeff and Desmond have experienced the many challenges and blessings of ministry in the kingdom. Their personal experiences both inspire their readers to get busy while humbly acknowledging the failures and trials that come with the journey. Although there are numerous helpful tools and antidotes offered to help in the process of revitalization and planting, I want to identify three that, in my mind, make this work stand out.

1. Personal illustrations of both success and failure. It humanizes the book.

2. Biblical models given to make us understand the challenges of those who have traversed these experiences before us.

3. Raw honesty that causes one to understand that failure is not in setbacks but in allowing setbacks to kill the vision.

This book can be a good source for anyone who is attempting a turnaround assignment, an assignment to bring health to a dying congregation or a church plant assignment. Those leaders will find honesty and vulnerability with tools to overcome and to get you victoriously through the challenges of contemporary ministry.

Dr. Mark J. Bane
Director of Evangelism and New Church Development
United States / Canada Region Church of the Nazarene

1

Living Again after Death

I HAVE HEARD PASTORS ask questions and make statements such as: Why are they always pushing church plants? I'm not interested in planting a church, I want to revitalize my church. Everything, including churches, has a birth date and a death date, nothing lives forever. We're closing more churches than we are planting every year. We have thousands of churches in need of revitalization; if we'd just focus on our existing churches, we wouldn't be closing them. These are all statements and questions heard in conversations from social media to board meetings, to denominational strategy sessions. We act as if church planting and church revitalization is a zero-sum game—as if we only have two choices, revitalize or plant. We act and talk as if those who want to plant churches have no concern for existing churches and would just as soon close existing churches since they are unhealthy. We talk as if revitalization and planting are completely unrelated, and it often devolves into an argument.

The work on this resource began on Easter Sunday. The day Christians celebrate Jesus being resurrected! Ironic, isn't it? Pastors who proclaim that Jesus rose from the dead to their congregations on this day, are often the same ones lamenting their church is dying. They seemingly forget that for resurrection to happen by definition it must be preceded by death.

Rise Again

Death and resurrection are modeled throughout God's creation. Every fall, plants and flowers begin to die and in winter seem dead. One glance across the landscape in winter and it reveals an almost lifeless, dreary, and barren desert-like earth. In just a few months' time that same barren landscape will rupture with flowers, grass, and new life. Violets will peep and buds will bloom as God renews the life of the earth. Just as the stone was rolled away from the tomb to reveal Jesus is alive, winter is rolled away to reveal the Earth is alive. The temperatures will warm, the sun will begin to shine again, and that same barren landscape will once again be a beautiful prairie of flowers and trees blooming and teeming with life.

I (Jeff) recently set fire to my yard. It was not an intentional act. A couple of branches were burning in my fire pit, the wind caught one, and began getting a little too close for comfort to the propane grill. Out of fear of the fire getting out of control, I removed the branch and tossed it in the yard, which itself immediately began to burn. I tried to stomp it out, but the wind caught it and it began to spread quickly. I ran to get the hose, but it was tangled. I ran to get a pitcher of water, but the faucet was too slow. Meanwhile the fire was rushing through my yard feasting on the buffet of dry grass, pine straw and bark. It was out of control! I called the fire department and in the short term took my little pitcher of water and dumped it on part of the fire. That pitcher of water was about effective at putting out a fire as a hoe would be at tearing down Mount Everest. Suffice it to say, thanks to a neighbor's heroic efforts combined with a fire department who arrived just in time, my house was saved—even though my neighbor's wooden fence was not. My fear almost caused a disaster. I feared the fire getting out of control. I panicked and made it worse. If I had just calmly walked inside and got a pitcher of water the fire would have all been contained in the pit and my bank account would have had a little more health.

Coming Back to Life

After this event, my yard was black. It was dead. No bugs and not even a worm could be seen inching its way along the ember filled yard. Last spring, I had paid a landscaping company to sod part of my yard where the previous owners had a trampoline. That was now up in smoke. It seemed whatever attempts I had made to have my yard look nice, were all for not. Then a funny thing began to happen as winter began to wane and the temperatures began to warm. Little blades of green began to peak through the black. A few more weeks of warm weather and more and more shades of green began to appear. It took less than two months after the fire that seemingly killed my lawn for God to resurrect it. It looks better than ever!

Witnessing Transformation

We even see this process of death and resurrection in some animals. In order to undergo its metamorphosis, the caterpillar buries itself in a cocoon for a period of time. While in its tomb (cocoon), it rests. This is the time God uses as a catalyst for its new life. Once the transformation is complete it bursts out and what emerges is a completely different creature. Had we not witnessed the transformation, we would have never believed that this beautiful creature that daintily flutters from flower to flower was previously a worm. We are immersed in reminders of resurrection every day if we simply open our eyes and pay attention. Knowing death must precede resurrection, why do we fear the death of our church so much? Perhaps it's the pain we fear? It is painful, often excruciatingly so as witnessed in the crucifixion. I have to remind myself that Jesus calls this birthing pains. We have only ourselves to blame for the pain. Remember pain during birth is a consequence of the fall. In fact, death itself is a consequence of the fall. Thanks be to God; Jesus provides us a solution to death. I thank God the pain is a reminder that I must repent in order to be reborn.

For some reason we can't take a hint. God is constantly reminding us that death is not to be feared. The message of Easter is Christ conquered death. As Christians, we do not have to fear death and neither do our churches. We pastors pontificate on countless Sundays that we need to trust God with finances, with trials, and tribulation; with all areas of our lives. We'll victoriously proclaim on Easter, "He is Risen!" But, privately to our peers, denominational and organizational leaders, and often out of sight of our congregations we lament that our churches are dying. We wring our hands, scour the web, and hire consultants to learn how we can revitalize our church.

The dictionary definition of revitalize is "imbue (something) with new life and vitality."[1] That sounds a lot like what we celebrate on Easter. Jesus, three days lifeless, was reinvigorated with life! He was renewed. He was given new life and vitality—resurrection! What we call revitalization God calls resurrection! Death is simply the first step towards resurrection. It is true of people, but it is also true of churches. Just as death and resurrection are part of the same process, so is church planting and revitalizing established churches.

Why then do we complain that there is "too much focus on church planting"? A church plant is new life and resurrection is new life. One small difference: a church plant has never lived. It is a new birth. A revitalized established church has lived and is trying not to die. Except the Bible says, "We are a new creation."[2] Baptism itself is a symbol of dying and being resurrected. From a biblical perspective, it seems that whether it is resurrection or a new birth, both are new life and God does not elevate one above the other or even distinguish between the two. Both are "new creations." If new birth and new creation are the end result, why do we fear death?

1. See the definition of "revitalize" at https://www.dictionary.com/browse/revitalize.

2. 2 Cor 5:17.

Grow in God

For a people whose God conquered death, it still seems to occupy too much of our thinking. Christian leaders are playing in the enemies back yard when they argue whether they should be focused on one or the other. As long as we're standing in our specialty silos of planting and revitalization, we'll never hear our brothers' and sisters' hearts. The distinction between revitalization and planting is really born out of fear.

Fear is a powerful tool, but it is not a tool that Christian leaders should ever use. As Christian leaders we must ask ourselves, would we ever consider casting a spell to revitalize our churches? Would we consider making a Faustian deal with the devil? Of course not! Neither should we use fear as tool. At its root the dualistic discussion between planting and revitalization is rooted in scarcity. In his sermon, "The Liturgy of Abundance, The Myth of Scarcity,"[3] Walter Brueggemann's thesis is God created out of "abundance," but we fear "scarcity." Brueggemann recounts the biblical story from Gen 47. The Egyptian Pharaoh dreams there will be a famine in the land. Out of fear Pharaoh hires Joseph to administer the abundance and take control of it to prevent the famine. The irony is that it is the Pharaoh's order to control the abundance that leads to the famine. In other words, the Pharaoh's hoarding of his abundance created his nightmare.

Arguing that there is too much emphasis on planting and not enough on revitalization is essentially a fear that there will not be enough people to evangelize. One glance at a George Barna study will tell you there is not a shortage of people in need of hearing the gospel. Our churches are hemorrhaging people. The pandemic struck an artery in the church and accelerated the bleeding of decline. While we stand in our echo chambers our churches are bleeding out and the community around the church is going to hell. We would argue that the church is committing the same sin as Pharoah. We are afraid of losing people and as a result we're creating that fear. Instead of preaching hope, we preach fear. Not intentionally. Yes, we

---

3. Brueggemann, "Liturgy of Abundance."

still preach the good news, on Sunday mornings most of the time, but that is not the sermon the vast majority of people are hearing. The vast majority of people are not in our churches. The sermon they hear is not from the pulpit on Sunday morning, but in our conversations as we go about our lives, in our social media posts, and even in the corner coffee shop as we wax poetic to our peers about the various ills of our churches. Those sermons are filled with fear and lament and without us ever knowing it, a potential new believer is turned off to the gospel. Those folks are just as screwed up as I am; I need hope not more of the same.

Nothing to Fear

Our American culture is drowning in images of fear—especially post pandemic. One could argue that the pandemic did more to divide us as people than anything in recent history. We were all driven to our silos; masks on or masks off; vaccinated or unvaccinated. It wasn't hard to find your silo. Both arguments were based in fear. One was a fear of the virus; the other was the fear of government control. But even before COVID, there was plenty of fear to go around.

Our entertainment drips fear. Alien invasions. Zombie attacks. Vampires and werewolves. Monsters in the closet. Monsters under the bed. And our worst fear is a monster who can't be killed! We've turned resurrection into something of which to be afraid! Recently while watching the newest iteration of the superhero movie about Batman, called *The Batman*, in the opening scenes Batman is narrating his strategy as uneasy music growls underneath. Referring to his "Bat Signal," the Batman says, "It's not just a call, it's a warning! To them. Fear . . . is a tool." The music gradually shifts to heroic. "They think I'm hiding in the shadows, but I am the shadows."[4] Since when do heroes use fear as a tool? Since when do Christians subscribe to fear? Do good guys hide in shadows and especially refer to themselves as the shadows?

4. See the full movie trailer for *The Batman* online.

Fear drives us to stay in our silos where we continually tell the same scary stores over and over again. Those horrific horror stories get echoed to each new generation. Stories about scarcity of life. Scarcity of money. Scarcity of resources. Scarcity of people. The planters want all of the resources. Worse, the planters want our people! Hands off!

I (Jeff) remember when I was planting my first church there were a couple of teens who were attending the church we had been attending when I sensed God calling me to plant churches. They had a heart for God. To be clear, we were not planting a church because we were angry at our current church. There was no animosity. Remembering one of those teens was gifted musically and the other loved people, we reached out to them to see if they would be interested in helping us get started. We would be meeting on Saturday evenings in the beginning so they would remain involved with their home church as well. It did not take long before I got an angry call from their pastor informing me that I needed to back off! I needed to find my own people. In retrospect, as a courtesy I should have let him know my intentions, but his was an overreaction to say the least. I backed off but those teens missed an incredible opportunity to see the kingdom in action. There is a reason the Bible tells God's people to fear not.

When we step out of our echo chambers and hear each other we learn those who desire to plant and those who desire to revitalize want the same thing. They both want the church to thrive and, in so doing, be a source of life for their respective communities. When we begin to plan together instead of arguing separately, we will discover that the same biblical principles which apply to revitalization are used in planting also. Church planting and church revitalization are both resurrections.

His Story Continues

God's story of resurrection echoes through eternity and into our lives. Resurrection can be a scary process, but I've witnessed enough resurrections in my own churches and in my own life to know if we trust God with that process, we'll emerge better and stronger than ever. If we will just listen to our own platitudes to "trust God" the church will experience a metamorphosis not unlike the caterpillars, the flowers in spring, and charred grass. Let's come out of our fear-based silos of scarcity, join hands, and work together to revitalize, plant, replant, and resurrect our churches in order that all people may "day by day, spend much time together in the temple, breaking bread at home and eating the food with glad and generous hearts, praising God, and having the goodwill of all the people. And day by day the Lord will add to our number those who were being saved."[5]

5. Acts 2:46–47.

2

Death to Life

Out of the Grave

FOLLOWING THE DEATH OF Jesus, the disciples hid in an upper room reliving the atrocities that had taken place in the last twenty-four hours. The sense of fear in that room was palpable. The fear of the unknown. The fear of things never going back to the way it was. A creak in the floor or a bump in the night had them on edge. That same sense of fear has been felt countless times around the church board table in established churches. As the church marches towards death the members understand that, without action, the church will be no more. The decline in membership, the lack of children, and disengagement in the community has led up to this point to death, but it did not have to end this way. For the church the decline happened over decades and for well-established churches all at once because of a moral or spiritual failure of a leader. If the story of Christ ended with the image of his disciples waiting out their fate isolated, cut off from the world, it would be a telling ending. Many established churches have waited, spent countless years isolated from the neighborhood, praying for a savior (a pastor, or program) to lead them from death into life.

In the waiting God can use the echoes of death to spring forth a resurrection in the spiritual life of the church and her members. It is in the waiting that God produces a vision for the remnant of believers to begin to pray through the peril of loss as they seek God's resurrection power. Like the disciples before, many church leaders are scared when a change season comes to even the most seasoned church member. When the winds of change blow into the church her leadership must ask themselves, "Are we willing to go through a near-death experience to experience the healing growth of faith?" Near-death experiences can jolt a church back to life as they mark the hard choices that lead to change, or on the opposite end to speed up death. Know this truth, even healthy churches must constantly find new ways to maintain the status quo, much less grow, because of the fickle nature of church attendance in today's culture. The church has begun to realize that death will come to all, but God is still wanting to revitalize the established church to reproduce healthy church plants and to come out of the grave as they grow into new life.

Jesus Is Alive, HOPE for the Church

If the story written about Jesus ended in a period, it would be a cautionary tale of leading from behind against the leading powers of the day. However, the story of Jesus was punctuated by God not with a period, but with a comma, that Jesus is alive, thus the story has an alternative ending. In Luke 24:34–49, Jesus appears to his disciples after he arose from the grave and shares that life has taken hold. While some Christians gloss over the story of the resurrection, or frame it once a year during Holy Week, the story should leap from the pages of God's word as it should resonate for the established church: there is hope, in what looked like the end.

Change Is Uncomfortable

Many people talk about change like it is nothing, yet change is uncomfortable when change comes to a person or even a church's life. It is inevitable that with change, there is pain and pushback. Pain comes from giving up on a person's desires for a stronger will, which causes resentment because of the changing nature within the church. This is seen through withholding tithes, small meetings rallying the troops against the change, families ceasing to attend services, and even outright insubordination by ignoring the change mandate and pretending it does not apply. It is a reminder that change is uncomfortable because it makes the church conform to a new season that some may not be ready to enter. With church revitalization it reestablishes the order of things within the church hierarchy and forces members to either let go or hold to the things they think matter to God. The alternative is staying the same and slowly losing members through death, as no new infusion of spiritual life is breathed into the church.

Instead of seeing change as a menace, leaders need to see change as necessary for future growth.

Change Is for the Future

Do you love old, well-established churches with a rich history? There is a joy in learning the history, the past challenges, and the God moments where something extraordinary happened. By understanding the past, you can see the future more clearly. Change is not for yesterday but for the day that has yet to come. Change should never be for change's sake, but change comes when a program or space has outlived its spiritual effectiveness in reaching the lost with the gospel. The church's focus is to be a missional outpost to spread the good news of Jesus. When the church turns into a social club focused on those within the four walls of the church and not the ones dying and going to hell outside the church's walls, then change must come. If the people attending the local church do not look like the people surrounding the church, then change must come. If more people drive into the church than live near the church, then change must come.

Change should be seen as a positive antidote to reclaim the church's health for future generations, not as death to what was in the past.

Change Is about Letting Go to Gain

The most painful part of a change season is when a person or family leaves because of the changes you have suggested and implemented. To know they left because of the change and not because God called them away pierces the heart more than they know. In these grieving seasons of loss, you must learn to turn that pain into prayer for the family who left and for the progress of the local church community. While prayer may not bring a person back, prayer sustains the lines of communication with God to make sure you are leading with his wisdom and direction.

Understand that God places the right people and leaders in the church for the needed season. Sometimes seasons are long, but others are short, and as a leader, and you cannot fear what season you are in. Remain in a season in prayer to know where and how God wants you to direct or serve in the local church. While some will go, know this truth; God will bring others into the church's fellowship that will help the church go to new heights like never before.

Change Is about Obeying God

As you read Scripture, you see a central theme that carries through the sixty-six books of the Bible, that is, obedience brings about God's blessings. When leaders missed God's best for their ministry, it was when they failed to be obedient to God's plans for their life. What about your local church? Are the people being obedient to God's plans? Have you led them in a season of prayer, discernment, strategic planning, and implementation? You might have lost some wonderful leaders in your time ministering in the local church. But what you see as a loss early on can become a gain to the kingdom when you see them flourish at another church and then see how God blesses your local church with new leadership who brought forth incredible abilities. Instead of fearing change, God wants you to obey his change.

While change can be scary and every loss painful, God always restores. Be reminded that the crucifixion of Christ did not rob the disciples from the resurrection of new life. In the flesh the disciples looked like they lost it all, but God had another plan. So too, when you keep serving God faithfully, he has a plan for your life and ministry.

Be encouraged to lean into a change season, do not hide from it because God is getting ready to pour out a storehouse blessing upon your local church if you are willing to face the consequences of leading change and resurrect the church from death to life.

Rebounding from the Grave

A new day brings about opportunities to renew the passion for the local church. Like most leaders you have felt the weight of a challenging season. With back-to-back years of pandemic-induced trauma, the church is slowly moving out of its protective cocoon to assess the damage left behind from the damages of COVID-19. For many churches, that means fewer people, less participation in church life by her members, and less income to help the church reach the community. But, with every dark season, there comes light in the dawning day before her.

Capture the Vision

The church's vision before the pandemic has changed due to the new realities before her. Instead of seeing the vision shattered, see it as an opportunity to reshape and then recast the vision to repurpose the church to reach the community where they are today. Far too many churches found out they were social clubs that closed or lost members during the pandemic. The pandemic exposed the promise found in man and not in God. For each season in the church's life, the vision has become recast to meet the needs for today, while the message of God's love and redemption remains the same. Today can be the day that the church captures a new fresh vision of serving the neighborhood around her and dreams about planting a new work.

Spend some time in the first part of your day and week talking with your neighbors, meeting new community members, and engaging current church members in conversation about where they see opportunities to serve the community and begin to lay the framework to recapture the vision for the lost. While some predict the established church will die, claim that your church will be healthy enough to plant a church in the future.

Create Opportunities to Serve

How often have leaders cast a vision in January and never mentioned it until the end of the year? Much like an exercise program or diet that is kicked off when the ball drops in Times Square, the program falls to the wayside over time without attention to detail, discipline, and determination. The vision to move out of the grave must move from the mouth into purposeful action where people are involved and invested. Do not stop at just one area of service. But offer a variety of places for your people to serve inside and outside the church. Much like the variety found out at a local restaurant, your people do not like the same thing. Play to the skill sets of your people through weekly interactions and long-term relationships serving together and provide the right community partners for them to connect to in the future.

Host a community fair in your fellowship hall and invite outside agencies and ministry groups to come and share their needs and provide opportunities for your people to ask questions and consider where to best serve. Make sure the commitment is limited to sixty or ninety days and then host another fair. This controlled commitment level enables members to know the time commitment needed. They can either sign up again to serve in the same area or with another organization if they like once the time commitment has been met.

Complete a Task to Gain Wins

Coming out of a season of disappointment, attaining early wins can build momentum for more significant wins down the road. As you develop relationships within the community, begin to invest in them, complete the task you've agreed on before moving on to the next project. How often has someone started but not finished a project in your house or even the church? Maybe that is you? Finishing a project or a task honors the commitment, but it also honors God by signaling that the church is ready for the next God project. Completing a task enables the body of Christ that you lead to celebrate what has been accomplished and to begin to dream again for what more God wants to do through your local ministry.

Wins are windows of opportunities to celebrate the volunteers that helped complete the task and opportunities to dream again. Celebrate the church's community partnerships through an exceptional Sunday service where agencies are highlighted. Have a giving Sunday where a special offering is collected by donating to a worthy cause through a member's choice voting—reinforcing that the church is there to serve, not to be served.

The grave seemed final, but Jesus' resurrection shows that nothing is final until God says it is final. God is calling the established church to rebound from the death spiral and to regain momentum to serve others in the community as they move forward to seed the spiritual ground for future growth and prepare the land for a future church plant.

Seeding for Future Growth

Recently I (Desmond) had the privilege of spending a few weeks with a substantial church that has seen strong and sustained healthy growth over the past twenty-five years. As I spoke to their tremendous leadership team, it was clear they had done many things right over the years, but it was not as clear if they could sustain the healthy growth for years to come. Like many established churches, they had early success, from reaching new families, expanding their building footprint, and programmatic expansion while maintaining a stable leadership team. Shifts in demographics and leadership change has forced them to see the need for a fresh vision to sweep over the campus.

As I was being shown around the campus my mind instantly wondered to fill in the missing gaps, as this church was good, but could be great. While it is the major transformations that get most of the praise and notice by attendees, it is the small changes that gain traction over time and lead to future growth. One of the questions I peppered my hosts with was what was their vision for the church for the next chapter she was entering? It was in their silence that I saw the need for strategic mapping that would lead to future growth.

Reposition the Vision

For many established churches they can look back on a time where the church saw sustained growth and allowed that growth mindset to lull them into a comfort that growth will beget growth. I asked one dynamic leader of the church to stand up on stage as people are entering the worship center and look out on the crowd and see which age groups enter the worship space. If the worship center filled with more folks fifty years and older than families with children, then the church had the early warning signs of future decline. While the church might look healthy today, with people in seats and tithes in the offering plate, within the next five to ten years the church will shift into a steep decline as the senior saints age if the church does not reposition the vision to reach younger families. Hear my heart, I am not suggesting that you ignore your senior saints; in fact, it's the pastor's priority to develop relationships and sustain continuity with them through special luncheons, visitation, and prayer meetings, just to name a few things, but shift resources to seed future growth over time. An established church can not plant a church if they themselves are already dead.

Resource the Future

In the church the leadership had recently decreased the children's ministry department budget and shifted those resources to other programs. While it may make sense on the outset to reestablish financial principles to make resourcing the church more equitable, the board in essence seeded future decline by removing the resources from the department. If the church is aging as I suspect by the data that was gleaned, then more resources need to be put into children and youth ministries to attract and retain young families with children. Observing the current space used by children/teens, the church leaders begin to see the space through their eyes. Design a space that is fun, educational, and spiritually strong. Far too many times leadership places their own ideas above the needs of those who utilize the space. Sprucing up paint, new furnishings, and design layout go a long way to providing a space where hearts can be won to Jesus. When you see the space through the eyes of a visiting family and not one who has been there for years, you can sow the seeds for future growth by mapping out a strategic plan to see the rooms filled with children's laughter or teens learning.

Replan the Space

The church I visited had this incredible gym that was used by multiple outside sources who are the untapped potential to future growth and a creative space for a future church plant or two. As I was strategically mapping out the space in my head, I was shown their kitchen and it was clearly inadequate for their current size and future needs. Next door to the kitchen was a classroom, where they could knock down the wall and expand the kitchen facilities to more modern use for future groups and church plants. This step would enable the leadership team to replan the space of the children's department to plan for future growth, as there were several underutilized classrooms that could be expanded or redesigned to fit their current and future needs.

In established churches many leaders get used to the current footprint and stop dreaming about what could be. Here this church sat on a beautiful campus with a small pond and picnic area near a playground. As the leaders shared that many in the community used the playground during the week, I envisioned enhancing the space by adding a second playground for toddlers, more shade trees, several walking paths with benches, and a new basketball court for teens to play on. While these changes may seem small, they will share with the community that others are welcomed here.

As the disciples embraced the fact that Jesus was very much alive, it created an opportunity to shift their outlook to see beyond their current circumstances to see where God was moving them. That shift created an indelible mark that the church follows today as they moved from death to life. If your local church is like the one described above, it is ripe for the harvest. If you are willing to seed for future growth through preparing your campus for use in the coming years and moving on from what it has been, you will set the church up for a God movement to come and be prepared to birth new ministries outside the campus grounds.

3

The Call

IN THE EARLY DAYS of my first church plant, Lisa, my wife, and I (Jeff) felt very much like the disciples must have felt once they realized Jesus was alive! But soon after Jesus' ascension, reality set in for the disciples as Rome was determined squash this new threat to the empire! The words "If you are not called to plant a church, for goodness' sakes, don't do it!" echoed in my ears, as if I were standing in the bell tower of the Notre Dame cathedral at noon soon after the excitement of my first plant abated. We had set sail on the voyage onto the ocean depths of church planting with great excitement and anticipation. We dropped our anchor in the deep, ready to do some serious deep-sea fishing. To say we had visions of grandeur would be an understatement. I had heard those words from mentors and other seasoned planters, but like a brash adolescent, I had not listened. We were naïve.

We struggled for a year to find people, a location, and a voice in the community. Despite my previous business connections, I was seen as a tech nerd, not a pastor. All my clients knew I was Christian, as we had many faith-based discussions, but that influence did not readily translate into having credibility as a pastor. The culture was highly entrepreneurial, and the value of the church was seen primarily as a networking opportunity to build one's business. A new church did not have much to offer a business-man or businesswoman looking for networking opportunities. We finally got some traction when we got word of a Bible study with some college-age people, and we were invited to share our vision. From that core group combined with some in-reach events in the community we launched with just over a hundred people. We were elated. I still remember my sermon on the "great commission." One member of my core team told me afterwards that it was the "best sermon I've ever heard on the great commission."

Monday came and we were feeling pretty confident, then the phone began to ring. "Pastor, I wanted to tell you how much we enjoyed the service Saturday night. However, this megachurch which we attended back home sent us a postcard in the mail. They are opening a campus in town and need volunteers. We're going to help them. I'm so sorry." On the phone I was cordial. Internally I was devastated. Judas might have come to my mind. Since my core consisted of a college group of peers, as one went, so did they all.

Within a month we were down to just our family and a cou-ple of faithful others. I think I set a record for destroying a church in the shortest period of time. Jesus had amassed huge crowds, but three years later, he died alone on the cross centered between two thieves and only his mother and one disciple at the foot of his cross, while everyone else hid in fear they would be next. It took me less than a month. As I said, I was a very naïve and too smug. At least I was not crucified, although at the time, the emotional pain to me seemed to be what I imagined was the physical pain Jesus experienced on the cross—difficulty breathing, questioning God, and feeling abandoned by everyone.

For the next two years we would struggle. Every day I ques-tioned my call. But every time God confirmed my call—not just in my spirit, but through others—through coaches, mentors, denomi-national leaders, and family. This was just all part of the planting process. I remember one planting coach telling me than the team with which you begin will most likely not be the team you have after the first year. Lisa and I had gone through all the training. We had been to an assessment where we received extremely high scores, and even gone through a marital and psychological profile. Throughout that entire process, which took over a year, my prayer to God had been "God, if this is not your will, stop me. Give me a no. Send red flags to my coaches, denominational leaders, and mentors. If this is not your will, I do not want to do it." I did not need to be a church planter. I was running a successful IT company at the time. Ministry was not my idea. I had sensed a call to youth ministry in high school, but upon entering college and in the midst of some spiritual confusion (Saint John of the Cross refers to this as the dark night of the soul),[1] I no longer sensed the call.

Preparing to Plant

I went on to start a business while in college that eventually became so successful I had to make a choice between running the business and going to college. Since that business was a maid service and I didn't want clean houses the rest of my life or find maids to clean houses, I chose college. Upon graduation I landed a job in Columbus, GA, not coincidently the hometown of my future wife. It was with a small business as an educational computer sales rep. I would be selling Macintosh computers to South Georgia schools. A few years later I purchased the business from my boss, and eventually became a Microsoft Certified Professional and transitioned the business into a computer network specialty company.

I did this for several years until I begin sensing God's call to ministry again. This time it was evangelism. I re-enrolled in a master's program for religion with a spiritual formation emphasis at Northwest Nazarene University. My religious reality was deconstructed over the next three years and in the end, I experienced a metamorphosis. God had been set free from the little cocoon in which I had wrapped him. This opened my mind, and I became curious. This curiosity was imbued with the courage to explore my faith and my assumptions about it and many other things.

1. See *Dark Night of the Soul* in Saint John of the Cross, *Collected Works*.

I now had a broader understanding of evangelism, which eventually led me to understand church planting is the most effective form of evangelism. Sunday school is effective. In-reach strategies, food pantries, immigration help, clothing closets, and thrift stores are all good ideas.

The Billy Graham Crusades had an incredibly effective ministry at packing tens of thousands in arenas to hear the gospel but if you want to reach the most people, church planting is the strategy.

All of this—my education, my sales experience, my entrepreneurial experience, the required adaptability and resilience I had learned, and even my personality—became the foundation of the skills God would use to shape me into a church planter. Those who knew me replied with a resounding "Yes!" when they heard I was called to plant churches. More importantly, those who assessed people and prepared people agreed. God called and the church had affirmed. Every time I doubted my call, God reminded me that he had been preparing me for this. So, for goodness' sake, if you are not called by God and affirmed by those closest to you and those your organization has assigned to assess your perceived call, do not plant a church.

Perhaps you are thinking, *Great, I'm off the hook*. I have been trying to tell people we need to focus on revitalization. From my perspective, since church planting and revitalization are part of the same process of resurrection, it is likely the existing pastor of a dying church does not have the skill set to revitalize a church either. Revitalization has its own set of challenges. There is overlap between planting and revitalization. Both are part of the resurrection process.

Both Require a Call

Just because you are pastoring an existing church that needs revitalization does not mean God has called you to do it. I know many denominational and organizational leaders who will look for a church planter to revitalize a dying church, because they share many of the same skills and personality traits.

Both Require the Pastor to Be Resilient and Adaptable

The fact is there are pastors who are excellent at pastoring existing healthy churches whether those churches are big or small (yes there is such a thing as healthy small churches despite our "bigger is always better" culture.) Those pastors will not always possess the necessary skill set to plant or revitalize a church. They are excellent leaders, but they are not excellent candidates for revitalization and planting. Some of these skills are certainly teachable and can be found in books, journals,blogs, and courses. A good mentor and coach are also helpful. However, some traits such as tenacity, passion, adaptability, and internal drive are more akin to personalty traits. A pastor who is accustomed to a healthy church will probably not have the patience for the chaos associated with planting and or revitalization.

Both Need to Be Change Agents

Part of being adaptable is having the ability to change and especially lead change. This is especially true for revitalization. Leading change is challenging. Existing churches have existing cultures. While attributed to Drucker, he never said culture eats strategy for breakfast, but it is true. In other words, just because a pastor or leader has an impeccable strategy that is logically sound and even well-researched, it does not mean he/she will not face resistance from the people. A church in need of revitalization is that way for a reason. Often the pastor who finds him/herself pastoring such a church is newly hired. Erroneously church leadership may have assumed that pastors who pastored a significantly larger church than theirs can miraculously make theirs equally as large. Even if that pastor had success growing an existing church, church growth and church revitalization are as different as an elephant and a tiger.

A change agent understands the difference between deconstructing a church's identity and shaping the church's identity. Deconstruction is a philosophical concept that is a product of our postmodern age, or some would argue it's simply the end or natural consequence of modernity. Deconstruction refers to work in the 1960s by the French philosopher Jacques Derrida.[2] It began by questioning assumed concepts in Western philosophy and recent years its rhetoric has found its way into the church. I would caution any pastor from utilizing such application in the context of revitalization. While it can be a powerful tool for shaping Christian thought in academia, the local church is not academia, and the pulpit is not the place for such rhetoric. That is not to say there is no room in the church for such discussions, but such a pastor would need to have a strong understanding of the personalities, culture, and systems of his/her church, a large amount of credibility and trust established, and finally a definitive idea of the new identity he/she plans to reconstruct. (Hint: it's called the *imago Dei*—the image of God.)

Credibility/Trust

Speaking of credibility and trust, while churches often seek a specific pastoral type with a revitalization skill set, a long serving pastor can absolutely learn the skills to revitalize a church. While he/she may not necessarily possess the personality traits of a planter and or revitalization pastor, he/she has enough credibility and trust that leading change would be much easier for such a pastor. In such an instance, hiring a coach and finding a mentor would be advisable to journey with him/her.

A Sense of Urgency

There is one key difference between a leader who is planting a church and one who is called to revitalize the church. A leader called to be a church planter is going to have a clear sense of urgency. Yesterday is not soon enough for such a leader. One who is called to revitalize a church will still have a sense of urgency, but it manifests in different ways and is paired with a strong dose

2. See Lawler, "Jacques Derrida."

of patience. (Anyone who knows me will tell you, patience is not one of my virtues.) There are instances where the change will have needed to happen yesterday. However, in the case of a long-tenured pastor, he/she has likely seen this coming for a while and has been subtly preparing his/her congregation. Therefore, a completely dismantling of the structures and systems of the church overnight is not advisable. Aircraft carriers take a while to turn and so do established congregations.

If most existing pastors of dying churches need a call and church planters need a call, what then is a leader to do? Seek outside assistance. As I mentioned before, one key to successful revitalization/resurrection is trust. Bringing in a specialty pastor often fails because he/she hasn't earned the trust of the congregation. There are different degrees of dying churches. I have known churches that run over 1000 on Sundays that are dying. Obviously, these churches will be a long time dying. The challenge for these churches is akin to the person who has early-stage cancer. He/she may be tempted to ignore some symptoms of sickness and procrastinate going to the doctor. However, over time the cancer continues to grow, and the symptoms get worse. These are the situations where an existing pastor usually remains in place, tweaks a few systems and practices, and readily turns it around.

No Time to Waste

Most churches are already in the throes of death by the time they realize they are dying. To continue the cancer metaphor, they are in stage-four cancer and the symptoms can no longer be ignored. For other churches, they were in denial for so long that they were sick—the cancer has spread to every other organ (system) of the church. It has become metastatic. These churches are in crisis and a church in crisis will often require drastic measures. A change in leadership is often needed. These are situations where denominational or organizational leadership have an acute awareness of the need and bringing in a church planter or revitalization pastor is advised.

Immediately after Lisa and I had gone through our church plant training and assessment, one of my mentors called us to help revitalize his church. In his case, when he was called to the church it already had cancer. There was hope it could be saved. The church had a reputation for conflict and had some strong personalities. His gift was conflict management. He was master at de-escalation and knowing when to let conflict play out (like siblings arguing) or when intervention was required (the sibling has a knife to the throat of the other one.) Obviously, those are meant to be facetious extremes. But this leader could teach a master's class in conflict management. Unfortunately, the leaders who were causing the conflict were not interested in reconciliation. They were more concerned with their personal power, and when he became pastor, they quickly realized there was no room for such attitudes.

One of my favorites of the twelve biblical principles we utilize at DCPI for planting and revitalization is the "boss principle."[3] Simply stated, the "boss principle" says that Christ is the Lord of the church and sets the agenda. Even after fifteen-plus years of planting and revitalization and a lifetime in the church, I am still gob smacked at those "Christians" who insist on being the church boss. These people are often the original "cancerous tumor" that spread. Unfortunately, excising the tumor at this stage often hastens the death of the church, unless we consider death is part of the process of resurrection, in which case we do not fear it. The pastor of the church who asked us to help them replant had excised the tumor, but there was a lot of "cancerous tissue" surrounding it which only left a handful of people.

We promised him six months but ended up giving him a year. We did not immediately relocate to the area where we were planting the church and it was close enough to drive. Our plan included a year of building relationships and doing in-reach events, while we met periodically with our core team. We fell in love with the people who were left and even though they were older, they had a will to live. They outworked us! With the lead pastor's ability to manage conflict and steady personality, combined with my

3. Wolfe, *Church Planting Essentials Full Handbook*, 9.

hyperactive and breakneck approach to change, it was a perfect match. Those senior citizens braved the hot, humid, southern August summer and went door to door inviting kids to VBS. From there we built relationships with their families, and the church had almost tripled by the time we left. We had several new families coming and a lot of new young people and children. We had two van loads every Sunday. The kids loved it! They felt like the senior citizens were their grandparents. Many had come from broken homes and didn't know their grandparents, and if they did, they were often very broken. The people of that church looked death squarely in the eyes and said, "Take your best shot!" They did not fear death because they trusted God with the hope of resurrection. "Where, O Death, is your victory? Where, O Death, is your sting?"[4]

Listen—Discern—Go

Both church planting and church revitalization requires a call; but there is room in the kingdom for pastors of all giftedness. Find your fit. The good news is that if you are a pastor and God awakens you to the reality that your church is dying, he has likely called you to play a role in its revitalization. It may require a mentor and or a coach, but if you are humble enough to admit your need, God can work miracles for those like yourself who are willing be his servants. It will be uncomfortable. Get accustomed to change and even some disappointment. It may require some experimentation. Desmond can talk about an Edison culture for churches. To paraphrase 2 Chr 7:14,[5] "If God's people, who are called by His name, will humble themselves, and pray, and seek His face, and turn from their wicked ways; then will He hear from heaven, and will forgive their sin, and will heal their land" (churches). Alan Hirsch recently stated in an interview with *Verge Network* out of Atlanta,

> As a spark is the potential for a flame, as a flame has the potential to be a fire, as a fire has the potential to consume

4. 1 Cor 15:55.

5. 2 Chr 7:14.

a forest, as a seed has the potential for a tree, as a tree has the potential to be a forest, but it's all contained in the spark, it's all contained in the seed, in potential. Every believer carries the potential for the whole . . . you look at any church, you see, this is a kind of a massive amount of seeds in here—every one of them has the potential to be a church and ought to be a church planter.[6]

This is a missional mentality. If we want the local church to survive, we must pray for such a worldview.

6. Hirsch, "Alan Hirsch: Sparks and Seeds," 00:06—00:25; 00:30–40.

4

The Power Problem

MORE THAN A DECADE ago, I heard the words for the first time, "Pastors will come and go, but I will remain here." It was a chilling reminder that the power lies not in the pastors' hands but the laypeople that the pastor is called to oversee in many cases. Each pastorate has been tricky trying to navigate these unspoken power bases. In reality it is a balancing act trying to develop strong relationships while listening and then finding out who the church's powerbrokers are within the early days of arriving. When facing power forces within the church, the pastor must either allow the fiefdoms to continue or shift the power dynamic to embrace a more significant role for others in the community of faith. So, what keeps established church pastors from not giving up? The short answer is, calling. When you look back at the church's history, you will find a group of people who prayed, sought God's will, and planted a church at a specific time and location. The church's address is not an accident, as God has had a plan since the beginning of time. God placed the calling on a person(s) heart, drew them to a location, and formed the church. While power within the church shifts between lay people and the pastor from time to time, the power of God's calling has not changed. He still calls churches to plant healthy churches and maybe he is calling you even now during a revitalization effort to begin to prepare for a future church plant.

As part of the preparation season, there are three characteristics in shifting the power back to God from mankind.

Instill Teachability

We define teachability as the growth of continual learning by using what is learned positively to help the church move forward. Through personal discipleship, the pastor teaches effective leadership traits from a biblical standpoint. The teaching is done not from a top-down approach but by coming up alongside another and communally serving with them. We have found that when you invest in others, they are more apt to be open to learning from you and then using what they learned in developing others.

In many churches, the dynamics can shift with a few key leaders being developed and then released to lead in their areas. Over time, the fiefdoms that once controlled the church will begin to soften and then crumble as these new leaders invest more and more in people within the church.

Empower to Lead

Every person within the church is passionate about something. Find the "something," and watch the church change in short order. I have found that people want to serve, but they are unsure of where or even how to help. When you empower people to lead in their passion, it leads to a revolutionary windfall of individuals and families who become invested in the church. In a day and age where families are becoming more disconnected from the local church, it becomes easy to get families to embrace the culture by allowing them to live out their giftings, thus becoming connected rather than disconnected.

Too many leaders try to dictate leadership instead of empowering others to take up the mantle of Christ. This trait is where leaders fail. Through personal or group discipleship, the pastor instills the church's values. Once the values are embraced, the pastor should encourage the people to go lead in their area of passion. Passion harnessed for Christ can power the church to a great future.

Execute the God Plan

Inside each person that sits in a pew or chair weekly is a gift from God to the local church. God has a purpose and plan for each person, and as a leader, you can shift the power dynamic within the church by allowing your people to execute the God plan inside them.

Recently a group of lay leaders asked me (Desmond) what my thoughts were on a children's play, and my fallback position was, "What do you want to do?" Because at the end of the day, I know that my giftings are not leading a play, but for these Godly people, it was their giftings. I wanted God's plan and purpose for them to be lived out by following their passion.

Think about it this way; what areas within the church do you need to let go of and allow others to lead? For me, I can't be the worship leader, office manager, children's teacher, janitor, greeter, and the pastor. However, many pastors try to or even feel that they "have to" be over all these areas. Execute your giftings by following God's plan for your life and the local church and allow others to lead in these areas.

If the church is going to represent God's best, then everyone inside the church must serve in the community of faith. Serving starts by surrendering one person's will for God's. The pastor instills teachability into the people through personal discipleship or strategies for discipleship by weekly teachings and small group investment. Once a group of lay leaders has been simultaneously developed, these new leaders need to be empowered to lead in their area of passion. In this stage, the pastor encourages innovation and even failure to enable newfound leaders to find their leadership feet within the church. The last step in shifting the leadership dynamic is to execute the God plan within the local church. What works for one church may not necessarily work for your church.

Find where God is leading, lead with him, and allow God to guide by obeying his calling for the church.

Overcoming a Barabbas Spirit

As the lobby began to fill with Sunday morning worshipers, I (Desmond) could hear a multitude of conversations as my office door was open. One voice in particular boomed over the crowd, complaining about how the breakfast station was set up, apparently not to this individual's liking. Each Sunday in established churches across America, the Barabbas spirit enters the church through her members. While the church should be a safe place for all who enter her doors, she has also become a place where the Barabbas spirit lives. In the Gospel accounts, we meet Barabbas, a prisoner of the Roman governor Pontius Pilate. Scholars believe Barabbas was an insurgent who was dissatisfied with the rule of Rome. Dissatisfaction within the church is not new, as newfound modern-day insurgents of change are trying to overthrow the future-vision leadership in the local church.

The world outside the church walls is shifting and changing with each passing season of life. For many in the established church, the only place they feel safe from the change is inside the walls. Thus, the Barabbas spirit comes to fruition when change arrives at their pew. Another man found in Scripture with a similar name is Barnabas, who had a different view of leadership. He led with his heart and was seen as an encourager to those he met. In challenging seasons in the church, leaders need to be more like Barnabas than Barabbas.

Be Courteous

What differentiates Barabbas from Barnabas is the character of the spirit. When faced with a difficult situation, the way a leader handles the issue speaks to the nature of the regenerated heart of the leader and the ability to lead effectively in all cases found in the local church. Sometimes this means ignoring the negative comment or addressing it in a respectful way and void of animosity. Sometimes people believe that not speaking harshly about a challenging situation is ignoring a problem when buying goodwill and time to react in a Godly way. Barnabas was known as an encourager, a courteous man of people's feelings even when he disagreed with them.

Social media has proliferated the ease of personal and partisan attacks behind the anonymity of a keyboard. The actions have filtered into the church. From chat rooms and private messages to conversations in person, the negative spirit has overwhelmed the established church; slowing or stopping the momentum for future change. The pastor has a unique vantage point to steer the conversation and actions in a direction that honors God by leading like Barnabas.

Be Christ

It is easy for a pastor to dismiss a grievance as another negative voice in the crowd of a revitalization effort within the church. Still, a Barnabas leader leads like Christ in all situations. Christ showed the early church through his actions to be empathetic to the pain that someone was in to be an effective leader, while at the same time pointing to the promise found in moving forward to a positive end. Even in his darkest hour, Christ pointed people back to God. It is easy to lash out at the Barnabas spirit that has come against your leadership, but Christ taught his followers to turn the other cheek. Through the love of Christ, leaders today are called to lean into difficult conversations and examine them with a spirit of respect for what the other side is saying. When facing a Barabbas spirit, the person wants nothing more than the pastor to be adversarial. Still, when you speak and act in Christ's love, it begins to disarm them and provides an opening for defusing the situation.

Be Continually Focused

Barabbas wanted nothing more than to disrupt the Roman officials' plans for the city. Even when faced with freedom for himself as the crowd was given a choice to pick either Jesus or him, he jeered the crowd into a frenzy that disrupted what should have been a peaceful process. In hearing the conversation in the lobby, I chose not to get up from studying my notes for the sermon that Sunday and gave them over to God. I determined that my heart and mind would not be overtaken that Sunday debating where a church member thinks a piece of our breakfast station should be placed. Instead, I chose to put my spirit into the hands of God and allow him to make a way forward.

There is a saying that leaders should not sweat the small stuff, and I would not allow one negative voice to ruin what God wanted to do that day. By choosing not to engage the Barabbas spirit, I allowed God to handle the situation and service. The service turned out to be one of the best ones we had had in some time. I do not think that was a coincidence because when you fully surrender to God, he will never let you or the church down.

While you may face a difficult person within the church, know that it does not surprise God. Instead, stay focused on what God has called you to do and keep loving and leaning into him. When a negative word comes your way, filter it through Jesus, and be the Barnabas God has created you to be.

Developing A Leadership Pipeline

According to an article from Lifeway Research, the average attendance of churchgoers in the church has dropped to sixty-five people across all denominations weekly.[1] With the church's shrinking comes the need to develop new leaders to create future lanes of ministry to reach more people with the gospel outside the traditional Sunday morning setting. There is a farm league in all major sports where athletes can hone their skill sets in a safe

1. Earls, "Small Churches Continue Growing," para. 3.

environment before they are called up to compete. Yet there is a tendency in the church to call someone up into leadership even if they are untrained because the church needs someone to fill the position.

With decreasing weekly church attendance, church leadership has to be more intentional in developing the leaders for the future—through three keys to creating a leadership pipeline.

Develop Leaders

Leadership cannot be limited to a certain age or gender but rather develop a cross section of leaders from all ages and genders. Inside the local church, there is the untapped potential of those sitting in the pew to lead a future class. Far too long, power within the local church has been controlled by a select few, and when those leaders either move on or pass away, there is no bench for someone to take their place. As the church adapts to the changing culture, the church leadership must better disciple a new generation of leaders. Mentoring is a crucial component of developing future leaders. Mentoring does not have to be structured, but it does have to be intentional where a current leader begins to create a new generation of leadership by taking them under their wing and showing them how to lead.

I am convinced that leaders are not born as much as they are developed over time through strategic development. The intentional investment made through personal relationships, opportunities to serve, and consistent feedback helps the future leader develop the skill sets necessary to succeed in service to the kingdom.

Develop Learners

Leaders need to develop learners willing to listen, learn, and lean into conversations to glean the most from them. While leaders can be fashioned over time, it takes the generous heart of the one called into leadership to be a lifelong learner. It is incredible how leaders took their knowledge for granted and forgot to pass it on. For a church to be triumphant, it needs leaders who develop learners with a heart towards service. Serving is not about a person or position but others. When you evaluate the ministry of Christ, you see that he developed leaders over time and not just by osmosis. He focused on finding individuals who were willing to die to rise in the Savior. The church needs those types of leaders who want to learn from others more senior in the position than them and to be able to admit when they do not understand something or why it is being done.

Learners who are willing to adapt to the changing culture and context of the local church community will be leaders who learn over time; they do not have to have all the answers. With a willing heart and an eye towards obeying God, the church can develop generational leaders who will embrace the church's change season and strengthen her.

Develop Life Lessons

As a leader begins to get their feet wet, they need to fail and be protected. When young leaders make a mistake, they are often chastised and chased from their position of authority. Instead of running off a new leader, embrace them by helping them understand where they went wrong and how best to have handled that situation. Senior leaders in the church have an opportunity to provide direction, protection, and a safe space to experiment as they grow into the leader that Christ has called them to be. Peter is one such leader who failed but failed in a way that Jesus was able to use his failings as a teaching tool to fail forward.

Like Christ before, senior leaders need to love their mentees with a devotion to make them better. Through long-term investment and understanding, the church's spiritual health will rise along with the leadership.

The church needs a leadership pipeline that develops leaders, learners, and life lessons that enable the church to raise future leaders from inside the four walls of the church. God is still working inside the local church, but if she is going to fulfill her true calling to make Christlike disciples in the nations, then she has to forgo the power struggles that many established churches face.

5

Every Church Planter Needs a Coach and a Mentor

LIKE OUR FAVORITE RECIPE of Grandma's, when we discover the secret ingredient that sets it apart, we want to replicate it. We want to mass-produce it and transport it around the world. We assume because we love it, everyone else will. Unfortunately, everybody's taste buds are different and may not always appreciate her recipe and its flavor as much as we did. The same is true for church planting strategies. Strategies are context specific. The strategy and approach that one planter has in Southern California may not be appreciated by those in Southern Georgia or even everyone in Southern California.

I (Jeff) was a worship pastor at a church in a small town in Alabama prior to being called to plant churches. This area thrived during the textile boom. There were cotton mills on what seemed to be every corner. Communities were not nearly as mobile then as they are now. "Mill villages," which were small homes built by the cotton mills for their employees and their families popped up in every community that became affectionately known as villages. Churches soon popped up in each village. During these times it was not uncommon for lay people to plant churches and for denominational leadership to encourage such activity (I wish they still did). Even though the communities had different names they were all probably within a ten-mile radius of each other. These communities all had very different cultures. If there were five planters planting five different churches in each of these communities, each would need a different strategy and approach. Be careful about making general assumptions about culture and context based on geographic location and close proximity alone. There may be nuances of which the planter is unaware.

When I planted my first church, I was in rural Alabama, but if one made the assumption that my city was like the rest of rural Alabama, they would have completely missed the context and probably failed to make a strong connection. They were even different than many other university towns. I grew up in a big university town, but the university was its own entity and while it had influence on the city's culture, the city had its own identity. Auburn's identity and the university's identity are closely linked. Many locals would say "most university towns are a university within a city"—Auburn is a city within a university. These contextualizations are a great example of why having a mentor who is ideally a native of the area in which he/she plants, or at least a connoisseur of the culture, is important.

Both the coach and a mentor are important relationships for the church planter. Neither the coach or the mentor is your best friend, nor should it be. Friends and family are important for the support system of the church planter. Those relationships can make the difference between the planter throwing in the towel and giving up or choosing to remain even in the darkest days of the journey. When my wife and I attended the three-day church planting assessment center we were in what seemed to be a fishbowl. Every conversation, every note we took was observed. I had to preach a sermon. We had to work with other people to formulate a plan to plant a theoretical new church. We both had to undergo psychological profiles. We had to participate in three different personality profiles and then had to do the same profile from the perspective of our spouse. In other words, the self-evaluation was how me and Lisa saw ourselves and the purpose of having us do the profile from the perspective of each other was to help each of us see ourselves from the other's perspective. Finally, we had an exit interview with a psychologist who gave us feedback on the observations throughout the week.

In the midst of all this, I had been diagnosed with gallbladder disease just two weeks earlier and had refused surgery in anticipation of this assessment which had been scheduled for three months. I was in excruciating pain. The assessors assessed both of us because it is imperative that the spouse is as equally capable and supportive as the planter. When God calls one to ministry, he calls both. Even if the spouse is not actively involved, if she/he is not supportive it will at a minimum be a distraction for the planter and at worst threaten their relationship. That does not even count the cost on the rest of the family and the church plant.

In his book *The Mentor Leader*, Tony Dungy, famed head football coach of the Indianapolis Colts, talks about when he quit high school football because he didn't like his football coach. His assistant principal invited him over to his house and convinced him to stick it out. Dungy returned to the team.[1] How would history be different were it not for a mentor in his life who convinced him to continue playing football? How would Dungy's life be different? I could tell countless personal stories and stories of others who planters and all walks of life who faced pivotal decisions. An inflection point in his/her life. A mentor, coach or family member convinced them to not give up and as a result their lives were changed forever. Often it is the planter who must learn to thrive and live before the church can thrive and live. I cannot honesty say I have ever heard the audible voice of God in a literal way, but I cannot count the times God has spoken through mentors, coaches, and others around me. There have been times I was in conversation with God, perhaps even resisting him, when a total stranger would say something that left me speechless. They had unknowingly confirmed something God was speaking to me. God's voice

---

1. Dungy with Whitaker, *Mentor Leader*, 211.

is not only herd in prayer. God is speaking to us every day if we just open our ears to listen.

The Difference Between a Coach and a Mentor

People often use the words coach and mentor interchangeably. Even secularists have begun offering "Life Coach" certifications, who are often more expensive and for some more attractive than a counselor. In a population who increasingly identify they struggle with anxiety; life coaches are increasingly in demand. When discussing the difference between a coach and a mentor, like most detitanations and even biblical interpretation, context is king. Words seemingly continue to shift in meaning, therefore nailing down a strong contextual definition is important. Context will give you clues as to the intended meaning of the word. In the context of church planting and revitalization, there is a small but important difference between a mentor and coach.

Mentor Me

A mentor is someone who has been where you want to go and is willing to help get you there. Here are a few characteristics of a mentor in the context of church planting. In a best-case scenario, the mentor is an expert on the planter's context. A mentor is in the trenches with the planter. He/she are deeply involved in the early staged of planning and strategy. However, the planter is deeply invested and interested in the planter's relationship with the Lord. The mentor may not be an accountability partner, but he/she does hold the planter accountable. A mentor relationship is like that of the rabbi's relationship with the students in Jewish culture. There was a saying in the Jewish culture, "Be covered in your rabbi's dust."[2] There was no higher compliment to a student than to follow so closely with his rabbi that they shared the same dirt. The relationship between the planter and the mentor should be almost

2. Tverberg, "Covered in the Dust."

this close. The mentor is as much a spiritual mentor as he/she is a mentor for church planting. The mentor asks tough, penetrating, and deeply personal questions of the planter. For this reason, the spiritual growth that arises from this mentor/mentee relationship reaps incalculable rewards for the planter. Finally, a lack of spiritual maturity in a church planter can destroy a new church. Reflectively, I can honestly say, my lack of success early in my church planting was in part related to my own lack of spiritual maturity.

Open to Grow into a God Leader

A coach is someone who has expertise in a particular area, in this case church planting, and can offer guidance, be a sounding board as the planter fleshes out his/strategies and provide a high-altitude view of the planter's efforts on the ground.

The coach is not as involved emotionally with the work of the planter. This is not to suggest the coach is apathetic to the planter's success and or failure. On the contrary, the coach to an extent has his/her own credibility at stake by partnering with the planter, which is one reason the coaching relationship and the person the planter engages is important and should be approached prayerfully. I have known high-capacity leaders and coaches who do not mesh with every leader.

The coach is primarily focused on evaluating the plan and strategy and not as much of a spiritual focus. The coach will primarily ask questions instead of give advice. In my opinion 85 to 90 percent of the coach's responsibility is to engage the planter's imagination. The coach encourages the planter to look at every possible angle of a problem before settling on a solution. This is one reason a planter needs to spiritually and emotionally mature. The process of being coached can be a high anxiety activity. It is understandable a planter can get defensive. It can seem as if the coach is picking apart the planter's plan and strategy. Remember the coach was hired to give you an outside perspective. It is like any other endeavor; we get emotionally attached to our own work and can make assumptions that we are not always aware we're making.

I call them bloodspots. The coach is not attacking the plan he/she is making sure you understand the assumptions you are making. If it is not clear to your coach it may not be clear to your team or even the group you're trying to reach. In the end, the planter's plan will be stronger and better. The coach asks strategic questions to the planter to cause more reflection and analysis from the planter.

In war there are commanders and generals. The commanders are on the ground directing the action and calling shots on the fly. The generals keep a close eye on the overall theater of war. In football there is the head coach and then your coordinators and or specific coaches for specific teams and or positions. When Paul "Bear" Bryant coached the Crimson Tide, he often stood in a tower on the sidelines so he could see the entire field of play. From his tower, he could see things the other individual coaches may have missed. Coach Bryant was known for being tough on his players and they respected him because of it. The coach challenges the planter and simultaneously encourages him/her.

Regular Conversation between the Coach and Mentor Are Encouraged

There are some areas of overlap between the mentor and coach. They are both intentionally investing the planter/leader. They both come alongside the planter, and both are concerned about the spiritual, emotional health, and maturity of the planter. For this reason, the mentor should have permission to share his observations with the coach and vice versa. Regular communication between the two should be encouraged and will ultimately make both more effective in helping the church planter achieve his/her desire outcomes. Perhaps a coach will be more focused on equipping and resourcing the planter as his/her contexts tend to be broader than the mentor. I'll say it again the mentor is much more focused on the character and spiritual life of the planter.

One primary area of overlap between the church planter's mentor and coach is they are both intensely interested in the discipleship plan and strategy for the church. The strength of new churches is they are necessarily evangelistic. However, the planter must be as intentional about his/her discipleship strategy as he/she is the evangelism strategy. Those who a new church reaches tend to be those who are in need of much healing. They often desire connection to God but have a distrust of the institutional church. Many have hit rock bottom and God is their last desperate attempt at life. Without a clear discipleship plan which is obviously biblically based and contextualized, the church is pointless and rudderless. The goal of church planting is not just to grow the church by drawing a crowd. The "Great Commission" is both evangelistic and disciple-making.

There are several good plans in existence from high profile pastors. Obviously, the Bible is foundational. Kevin Myers, founding pastor of 12Stone Church, wrote a a book entitled *Home Run: Learn God's Game Plan for Life and Leadership*. In this book, which is actually based on a sermon series about discipleship, Kevin uses Rom 12:1–2 to develop the analogy of a baseball diamond as the pattern for discipleship and life leadership. He is, however, not the first pastor to envision a diamond shape for discipleship. Rick Warren uses the same analogy of a baseball diamond to illustrate his "Purpose Driven Life." There are others out there—I suggest you look at all of them and modify them for your own context, while giving credit to the original source. I am not saying to use it as is. The planter will have to contextualize the discipleship plan for his/her church and one's coach and mentor can help him/her. I prefer to be original and create my own, but my wife has a PhD in curriculum and not every planter has access to that resource.

Get Up and Walk

In John 5 (NRSV) Jesus heads to Jerusalem for a feast. When entered the sheep gate, which we now know as the pool at Bethesda. When he encountered the invalid, he complained to Jesus that he couldn't get into the pool and had been there thirty-eight years! Jesus replied to him, "Do you want to be made well?" (v. 6). Again, the invalid explains all the reasons he couldn't get well. Jesus replied simply, "Stand up, pick up your mat, and walk" (v. 8). There will be plenty of excuses for the planter to fail. There will be plenty of opportunities for pity parties. The one thing you as the planter cannot afford to do is sit around and play victim. Often your family will empathize. Your mentor will probably sympathize. Your coach will tell you to get up and walk! Life is hard. Planting a church while simultaneously living life is harder! The statistics for a new church plant are basically the same as they are for a brand-new business just starting out. According to the Bureau of Labor Statistics, over 20 percent of small firms fail during the first year of operation. Thirty percent of enterprises will fail by the end of the second year. Approximately half of the businesses will fail before the conclusion of the fifth year. By the end of the decade, only 30 percent of enterprises will be left, representing a 70 percent failure rate.[3] The rate for new church plants is 80 percent.[4] The reasons are many, but the fact is only 30 percent survive. One of the primary reasons for church plants failing is the planter quits. I get it. The burnout rate for pastors is already high and a parachute drop church plant and the stress level can be unbearable—except for the mentor and coach and of course God, which will eventually lead us in our discussion of the "secret sauce."

3. Carter, "True Failure Rate of Small Businesses," para. 3.
4. Baptist Press Staff, "Study Suggests New View," para. 12.

6

Called to Lead with Others, Not Alone

THE CONCEPT OF PLANTING with a coach or obtaining a mentor is the same side of the coin in the arena of church revitalization. The model of coach and mentor is not new. In fact, it is as old as time itself as it was revealed in the life of Jesus Christ. Throughout his earthy ministerial service, Jesus would pause and invest in people and places that were not seen as valuable to outside the class structure. But God was able to use the ordinary to do something extraordinary and he can use you. The journey of ministry is hard enough but trying to do alone is giving up one of the greatest assets a pastor can have, partnership. You cannot enter church revitalization blind. You have to be willing to partner to sustain your ministry.

You Think You Are Called to Church Revitalization

Ministering after a once-in-a-lifetime pandemic is difficult, but add to that ministering in a more secular world than any time since Jesus, and it almost becomes overwhelming. One can understand why pastors walk away from ministering in the local church. For over a decade, I (Desmond) have assisted and served in established churches trying to rebound from decline. The work of church revitalization is not just for one denomination to access but is desperately needed across all denominations. The established church is feeling the effects of negative attendance and offering numbers. Where once endowments would slow the decline of closing churches, the cost of deferred maintenance on older properties is stripping away the financial safety net and exposing the need for church revitalization as growth has become anemic at best.

There are twelve keyways to know if a person feels called to church revitalization that I have found in coaching others through church revitalization. This list, while not exhaustive, is definitive in allowing the pastoral candidate to know if they have the skill sets needed to lead a turnaround in an established church.

1. **Be willing to pray for others and God's dreams for the church.**

   God has great plans for the local church. It is not by accident but by divine appointment that God led planters to plant the local church at its current address. As the established church began to decline, its members became fearful and missed what God was doing in their midst. Their focus became on their needs and not God's direction. God can restore what the enemy has stolen through intentional times of dedicated prayer. Prayer ushers in God's spirit and sweeps out the negative image of where the church is today to where she can be tomorrow.

2. **Be willing to learn from others inside and outside of the church.**

   God has a specific plan for the church today, and while the church should celebrate her past, she cannot stay there. What worked ten or even five years ago may not work today in the context of where the church is at this moment. An adaptive spirit must be viewed with openness to circumvent years of inside-focused ministry and see God's new plan outside the church. The same programs or style of music of the past may not be the style needed today. The voices of church and community members should be listened to and sifted through to glean wisdom through discernment from God to find out what is needed to minister today to God's people.

3. **Be willing to say goodbye to say hello to new people inside the church.**

The hardest part of change is saying goodbye to those who resisted the change. Do not hang on to people or what holds God back from his plans for the local church. Instead of chasing after those who leave the church, permit them to go. Pray for them and release them into the community as missionaries from your fellowship. As you release others, be sure to invest in potential members found in your daily interactions in the community. See potential members from your barista at the coffee shop to the front clerk at your doctor's office. While you will lose people in a changing season, God has new people to replace them.

4. **Be willing to adapt to what is working and what is not working.**

Being willing to examine everything from programs to positions inside the church is essential for your leadership as the church prepares for the next season she is entering. For far too long, many churches have held on to what is not working because it had worked in the past. Evaluate every program and position for gospel effectiveness. With the church having limited resources (people or finances), instead of holding onto outdated programs, celebrate what has been accomplished and close them out as you announce what will come in the future. Remember, God has the right people and programs for the new season your church is entering if you trust him.

5. **Be willing to find joy in the simple pleasures around the church.**

In a revitalization effort, discouragement will abound. Entering a changing season causes others to push back against the impending change. The cycle of change and pushback can cause discouragement and resentment if the leader is not careful. At the beginning of each day, write down three things from the day before you were thankful for and hold on to those thoughts as you enter the change space. Write on a sticky note at the end of the day and leave it on your desk what you were thankful for today. It can be as simple as the flowers blooming outside to writing no disagreements today. When you come in the following day, you will see the note and remember that you are making progress, even slowly.

6. **Be willing to take criticism as part of being a change agent.** Change creates a critic in everyone. To sustain forward momentum in your ministry, you will have to absorb criticism and release back in a positive way into what you have been called to invest your calling into. As a leader, you have a clear vision and passion for seeing it completed. But not everyone inside or outside the church will agree with God's vision placed inside you. There is an old saying, "Like water off a duck's back." Realize that water does not soak into the duck feathers because of its oils; you have to have spiritual oil to release what is not of God; ignore the behavior as you move forward. God has a perfect plan for your ministry, but the evil one wants nothing more than to discourage and dissuade you from moving forward by drowning you in a negative chorus of voices. Find ways to stay positive by staying the course as you move forward.

7. **Be willing to partner with others outside of the church.** As a revitalization leader, you will learn quickly that you cannot do it alone. The church cannot do it alone. If the church is going to move forward, its members must get outside her four walls to connect with the community around her. The easiest way to gain traction with limited resources is to partner through volunteerism with a non-profit agency in the community. Many nonprofit organizations lost volunteers and donation base during the pandemic and would be glad to receive your church's help.

Also, find other pastors, even outside your denomination, by being intentional in having a meal together or sharing coffee. You will be surprised at how these monthly outings can rejuvenate your soul and show you are not alone in ministry.

8. **Be willing to find new ways of doing ministry.**
Your local church may be holding on to past programs, but if they are not effective for winning the lost today or growing stronger Christians, they must be retired. Most seminaries and Bible colleges do not offer courses on reviving declining churches, but the business world has many real-world examples of leading a turnaround. The skill sets that can be gleaned from the business world are developing a plan, being creative, implementing the project with enthusiasm, and adapting when change is not working.

   Sometimes new ways of doing ministry may be the same program but a different delivery or style. Know your local context and develop a way forward that is God-centered and God-anointed with your people.

9. **Be willing to find and share the story of Jesus in the community.**
Everyone has a story to share. Even the negative voices inside the church are sharing a story of pain and loss from the revitalization effort. Be willing to highlight stories that show the redemptive power of Jesus Christ as life change in a person's life. The stories of redemption will become stories of restoration for a church desperate for a win. As you go about your daily routines, look for accounts that you can incorporate into your sermons or personal conversations with church members. For far too long, the story of your local church has been death. Begin to speak life back into your fellowship by telling stories of life change.

10. **Be willing to stay put when things get hard inside the church.**

    If you want an easy assignment, a dying church that requires revitalization is not what you need to apply for. But, if you want a church where you can see the hand of God move, be creative with space and programing, love the history of older places, and have patience, then church revitalization might be your calling. The work you will do inside the local church will be challenging, but spiritually rewarding, if you are willing to surrender your will for God's will and not give in when it gets tricky. Remember, the church did not decline overnight and will not rebound quickly, but you will become the majority that can lead to the church's turnaround with God and key leaders who share the God vision inside of you.

11. **Be willing to find rest in your personal life outside of the church.**

    The work you will enter will be mentally and spiritually exhausting. It will deplete your soul if you do not find ways to rest. I cannot challenge you enough to find dedicated times of rest throughout the week and to have planned getaways not connected to the church. I have seen a minister's faults and personal failures overtake the positive work they are trying to accomplish because they are tired, and their judgment becomes suspect. Resting from the work of the ministry will enable you to evaluate the current needs of the church (positive or negative), provide you needed clarification of your own spiritual life, and give you a new perspective on your mental state as you move forward. An exhaustive state instead of a fresh mindset is the groundwork for spiritual failure. Stay fresh and find times to rest.

12. **Be willing to stay positive in all situations.**

    You will be your most prominent advocate or adversary. While you will not be able to control those around you, you can control how you react to every situation that comes your way. Every day you will be faced with joy stealers, but only you can give away your joy from your spirit. Be a joy keeper by finding joy in the daily routines of ministry. God has called you to your current ministry assignment, and only God can release you. Stay prayed up, listen to the call from God, and keep moving forward until he tells you to stop. The best days of your ministry are ahead if you are willing to find joy in small and big things while serving in ministry.

Leading with a Team and Not YOU Out Front

Planting or revitalizing a church are some of the most challenging grounds a leader tries to cultivate. Serving alone or with a super-human mindset instead of spirit-led can lead to personal and ministerial destruction. Every year a couple of high-profile ministers fall from grace because they have not developed a team that holds them accountable for their daily actions. While the high-profile leaders gain the headlines, this situation is played out in countless communities across all denominational sectors on a smaller scale. Serving in ministry is challenging but operating with an "alone mindset" can be spiritually deadly. The Christian church has learned that when leaders lead out front with no accountability, they become spiritual targets of the evil one. So how can the local church reverse the downward spiral of lead pastors who fall into the temptation of sin?

Accountability for Short- and Long-Term Actions

As a leader your ministry's results are seen not only on Sunday mornings but behind the scenes as they play out during the week. God has called you into meaningful work—work that the evil one wants to stop or destroy, so God's people do not win that ground. Stop for a moment and think about who is around you as a leader? Who you place around you during a leadership season is as important as who you have not chosen to be around. Far too many leaders want people who say "yes" around them rather than having someone who supports their leadership but is willing to question steps when they disagree.

Without proper accountability and the ability to have others speak into you and your ministry, you are harming the witness of Christ and jeopardizing your church's future. Accountability should not be a bad word, but a word that speaks to dialogue, robust back-and-forth, and a prayerful understanding that God needs to be glorified and not the leader. When you permit a handful of Godly laypeople or pastors to speak into your ministry, you enable the spirit to work through them to help improve the church and, by default, your ministry. Instead of being uncomfortable, be comfortable with rebuking and tough conversations as you realize it is done in a way to help and not harm the church.

Accurate Feedback from Someone You Trust

Scripture teaches that everyone should have the opportunity to share their concerns or praise regarding ministry issues inside the local church. But not everyone should be permitted to speak about the ministerial journey of the church as it relates to your spiritual leadership of the church. The church has an established leadership structure, not for hierarchical purposes, but because it is biblical. It enables the pastor and lay leadership to prayerfully consider all avenues before they are brought forward to the church membership.

Throughout Scripture, Godly leaders had a small group of advisors who had permission to speak truth into a leader's life. That truth was done out of love and not out of harm. They were done in private and in a respectful tone. However, in today's world, too many people feel they have a right to speak about all subjects in any manner they wish. Through the advent of social media, people have permitted themselves to comment on everyone and every subject under the sun as self-described experts, which is not biblical and is worldly harmful. When a leader puts people into leadership that they trust, it provides an extra level of openness to receive what the other person has to say. A strong biblical leader understands that feedback from all areas of their life is essential but sifting through it becomes the key to attaining the proper level of feedback about a situation.

Acute Awareness of Your Strengths and Weaknesses

Do you know your strengths and weaknesses as a leader? Leaders fall not because they woke up one morning and let themselves sin. Leaders fall because they failed to put safeguards around their weakness. Think about it this way. If you love chocolate, it is not one piece of chocolate that will harm your health. So, chocolate once in a while is okay. But having chocolate by the handfuls multiple times a day will affect your health. One handful of chocolate (sin) could destroy your ministry when you equate that to sin and ministry. When you know your weakness and areas of gifting, you can provide safeguards. Think about it this way; a leader is only as effective as those around them. As a leader, you must understand that you cannot know everything about every subject. Still, you can permit a small circle of people who are experts in certain areas of your weakness and can pinpoint problematic issues before they become problem areas by speaking the truth to your spirit.

Leading with a team and not you is hard for leaders, but leading alone can cost you your relationship with Jesus. Turning around an established church or planting a new church is hard enough but doing it alone or with limited support can destroy what God is trying to do through your ministry. Do not be ashamed to admit your weakness and be comfortable asking for help. As you understand who you are and build a team of trust around your ministry, God will begin to offer more opportunities for effective ministry. But do not be surprised if you are not tested and targeted by spirits and people who want to stop the God calling on your life. Safeguard your ministry today by praying for God's direction and wisdom and who to ask to partner with you in revitalizing and planting churches.

7

Secret Sauce

OFTEN, THE SECRET INGREDIENT to Grandma's recipe is the sauce. A good sauce can take a bland recipe and add zeal. It can take the ordinary and make it extraordinary. One of the things that almost every pastor of a church in need of revitalization and church planter longs for is a secret sauce. Something that will magically resurrect their church and cause it to thrive. Something to give their previously ordinary church new zeal and make it the talk of the town as news of its new flavor spreads. Or in the case of a church plant, this secret sauce will cause it to explode in relevance with people overnight. Volunteers will stand in line for a sample of its flavor, and even beg for a slice to share with friends. Finally, after seven chapters we're ready to share this secret. It is exactly the very thing that will give then "new wine for new wineskins" (Matt 9:17). Honestly, I'm not sure why it is such a well-kept secret. It is in plain view and is mentioned throughout the Bible. I'll confess, I missed it too even though my grandfather told me and showed me throughout his life. Without this secret sauce, you will fail in your mission and vision for your efforts to revitalize or plant your church.

I (Jeff) told you earlier that you were already in trouble if God had called you to plant a church and the same can be said for revitalization efforts. While both are part of the resurrection process God uses to transform your church, each one has some unique challenges. The challenge in planting a new church is that you have nothing. You and Jesus are the main attraction along with the vision God gave you for his church. Your plan must encompass everything, and you must try to identify all the landmines and avoid them. In the beginning there is not one but you, God, and your family. Pastoring already has a high burnout rate and lonely. Church planting can increase these feelings of isolation.

Turning Around Normality

The challenges of revitalization are also many. The positives are the pastor already has a congregation; he/she probably already has a building, and hopefully a ton of trust and credibility built up with the congregation. But those positives can just as easily be negatives. A building can become a cross for the congregation to bear that a previous pastor, with a bigger congregation, over built, and went deep into debt. Something happened. Perhaps a major donor(s) who had pledged support became angry and left. Maybe, a congregational split occurred. Building programs can bring out the worst in people; one's personal preferences quickly become confused with necessity and couched in religious rhetoric to justify one's position. Regardless of the reason, without tithes and offerings this building of blessing becomes a cursed idol putting pressure on the pastor and congregation. An existing congregation has an existing culture. The words commonly attributed to Peter Drucker, "culture eats strategy for breakfast," have become a mantra for leadership. It simply means that a leader can make detailed plans, using well-researched and resourced ideas, but the culture of an organization will ultimately decide the direction, and as any leader with real world leadership experience can tell you, the direction determines success or failure of strategy. In the case of revitalization, the church was already headed in the wrong direction, otherwise there wouldn't be a need for revitalization.

Often the existing culture is toxic when a church requires revitalization. There are, of course, exceptions. If there is one thing I have learned from twenty years of planting and revitalization along with eight years of post-college education, it is to not speak in absolutes. A good leader learns to look for nuances in understanding because often those nuances revel the root cause of a problem. One of the challenges of our current culture inside and outside of the church is a failure to recognize nuances because social media has created echo chambers of like-minded people which cause us to live in alternate reality without being exposed to alternate viewpoints. This creates blind spots. I have heard church planters envy pastors who revitalize churches. As a pastor who has done both, I prefer to plant. I'm sure I have blind spots; every leader does, which is why we need coaches and mentors, but one thing I know about myself is that I am not a patient person. I struggle in the context of revitalization when the people are resistant to change. The pressure of time, money, and even survival quickly leads me to frustration. I compare this to a person who is diagnosed with clogged arteries and surgery is suggested to remedy the problem. The person refuses and risks further heart damage, including death, all the while praying for a miracle. Sometimes, the miracles God provides are the people he places in our path to give a solution to our problems.

The point in all of this is to say that planting and revitalization are hard! These pastors are the special forces of the kingdom. If heaven had Army Rangers and Navy Seals, these leaders would be in that elite group. They are resilient personalities. They are battle-hardened and ready for combat on a moment's notice. They go places even some angels fear to tread. God has equipped them for this specific work. Many would not do well in a healthy church context because they are accustomed to crisis mode. Times of crisis require unique leaders and unique skills. The pressure is extreme. The enemy does not cede ground easily. Planting and revitalization are the front lines of the war between good and evil, and the enemy wastes no time in making a full frontal assault on the family, the planter, and even extended family. The enemy is cunning and will do and say anything to distract the leader. I've seen moral failure, I've seen sickness, I've seen discouragement, even the mind of the leader him/herself. Even in existing churches, this secret sauce is the key ingredient.

No Spoon Feeding

Without getting too far into the weeds there are basically two pedagogies in education. One is positivistic and the other is constructivist. An educator or leader with a positivistic view believes he/she has the knowledge, and the learner is essentially a blank slate or an empty vessel waiting to be written upon and filled with knowledge. If only it were that easy! The constructivist believes learners construct their knowledge through a variety of means such as experiences (good and bad), observations, inherited beliefs, stories, and more. The learners may have incorrect knowledge or incomplete knowledge. Thus, the responsibility of the educator is to shape this knowledge by allowing the learner to discover these answers through the guidance of the educator. The learner will research, listen, work cooperatively with others, and use other means in the construction of this new knowledge to build upon his/her existing foundation.

In Christian circles we use the term "spiritual formation." In the context of an existing congregation, they have likely had many pastors over the years and arrive on Sunday morning with those pastors' words echoing in their ears, and bouncing around in their minds, along with the stories of the politics of the world, work, and the pressures that exist in all those contexts. This is the environment in which they are constructing their knowledge which is creating the culture of the church.

I want to take you on a journey of discovery to help you construct new knowledge. I am not interested in deconstructing your existing knowledge to fill you with the right answers. You have enough deconstructing going on and it seems not enough people are willing to help reconstruct it. I'm not sure they know what they want to build or at least if they do are afraid, you'll resist if they tell you. When a learner discovers the answers for him or herself, they tend to take root. I want you to appreciate the wisdom of this secret sauce so you will not make the same mistake that I often have and take it for granted or ignore it all together. I believe you are smart enough and capable enough to learn from my mistakes and pay attention to how prophets, disciples, kings, and even Jesus used this secret sauce and how it made all the difference.

The Daniel Model

Our first leg of the journey takes us to the prophet Daniel. I find it interesting that most children's stories depict Daniel as a young man when they tell this story. He was not. Scholars believe he was about eighty years old when he was in captivity in Babylon. Daniel was not a neophyte; he was a seasoned prophet. He had lived long enough to acquire much wisdom and that wisdom helped him discover the secret sauce. We will join his story in Dan 6. King Darius had appointed 120 satraps (governors) over the kingdom and three presidents, of which Daniel was one. Because Daniel was faithful even in his service to an enemy king, he had risen to the top. Despite the others' best efforts to catch him stealing or doing wrong, they had not. He was above reproach in everything he did. Imagine having someone looking over your shoulder, watching everything you were doing. Imagine that pressure. He was already in a hostile kingdom. The others were jealous of him and desperately wanted to catch him doing something wrong.

The Scripture tells us Daniel was neither "negligent" or "corrupt" (v. 4). In other words, he wasn't lazy or derelict in his duties and performance as a president and he did not cheat.[1] It would have been easy for him to do it. He could have justified doing just enough, but he excelled in his performance to the point that he was favored by Darius. He could have justified cheating. Darius had plundered Israel, and much of his wealth was ill-gotten gain. However, they finally caught Daniel on a technicality. Daniel was faithful to his core to the LORD even as he served Darius and the others knew that fact.

---

1. Dan 6:1–4 NRSV.

Daniel is a model for how we can be citizens of the kingdom of heaven while simultaneously being a witness to the kingdoms of humanity. Unless the laws of the land and rules of the earthly kings were contrary or in opposition to the LORD, he faithfully performed them. But he would not compromise his relationship with the Lord. Even though he had signed a document pledging his allegiance to Darius, a requirement unless he wanted to immediately have his head permanently removed from his body, he continued to kneel, face Jerusalem (the location of the temple, thus YHWH), and pray three times a day. We are told he would "Pray to his God and praise him, just as he had done previously."[2] They had him! They reported this to Darius, and he had no choice except to execute by feeding him to the lions. He would lose credibility as a king. I am fond of learning lessons from bad leaders too. We can learn what not to do. Sadly, many of the lessons of leadership I have learned I learned by watching bad leaders make mistakes and making a note to lead differently. When we use fear as a tool to control and lead people are not joyfully serving and the first sign of weakness or indecisiveness you will be dethroned as a leader. Darius did not want to execute Daniel and looked for every loophole but ultimately, we are told, "Then the conspirators came to the king and said to him, 'Know, O king, that it is a law of the Medes and Persians that no interdict or ordinance that the king establishes can be changed."[3]

You know the rest of the story. Daniel was tossed into the lion's den by Darius, but God rescued him from the mouths of the lions. They became pussycats in the presence of the Lord's faithful prophet. Darius was overjoyed and Daniel's accusers along with their families were tossed in and were immediately killed by the lions. The thinking was Daniel had been proven innocent, so the others were assumed to be guilty of lying to the king. If they were innocent, they would also be spared. Not only did God save Daniel, but because of his rescue, Darius made a decree that "Daniel's

2. Dan 6:13 NRSV.

3. Dan 6:15 NRSV.

God was superior to all other gods."[4] Often, we think prayer is inconvenient. I am a man of action. I am continually tempted to dismiss prayer. I have been known to say, "We are the hands and feet of Jesus in the world, he accomplishes nothing without the cooperation of his people." I told you I am impatient. Prayer can seem laborious to me. It can seem like I am wasting my time. I tell myself I need to be in the community building relationships. I need to be planning. I need to be working the plan. I need to be preparing my sermon or writing my next book or article for publication. Daniel is a reminder we can do both. Before we jot one letter on paper, take one step towards fulfilling God's mission for our church; before we speak one word of advice to anyone, we must first be on our knees in prayer. It is not an optional activity.

Daniel had witnessed this. He had learned from the bad leadership of others. The previous generations to Daniel had a pattern. God would lead them out of exile into the promised land they would thrive. They would become comfortable, began to drift, and would eventually falter, turn away from God, or begin to trust in themselves and other gods because they became insecure in their own identity as the covenant people of YHWH. They kept looking at their neighbors' big militaries and bigger kingdoms and kept desiring to be like them. They stopped praying to YHWH and started praying to foreign gods and that always led them to trouble. Once they began to trust in things besides God, they would find themselves being conquered and led into exile. They had fallen and couldn't get up! This did not happen just once; it happened over and over again. Their leaders made bad deals with other kings despite God's warnings, and it always led to failure. Once they were in trouble, they would of course turn back to YHWH and he was faithful to forgive and rescue them once again. Daniel had seen the consequences of compromise and a life without prayer and learned those lessons well. As a result, God was faithful to rescue him from the mouths of the lions.

4. Dan 6:26–27 NRSV.

The Joshua Model

Our next step in the journey finds us with Joshua, as the children of Israel were being led to the promised land. Remember God had promised them a land of their own, but other people owned that land. Technically it was occupation, because ownership in the sense as we understand it today did not exist. Nation borders existed until another nation who was stronger (or, in their view, another nation whose god was stronger) invaded and kicked you out of the land. The idea that a group of refugees would somehow succeed in crossing a desert and defeating other king's armies to take the land God had promised them was about as absurd as thinking Mexico would rise-up and take the United States. But God had led them to the impenetrable walls of Jericho, and it was next on God's list for them to conquer on their way to the promised land. Jericho was part of Canaan, and they were one of the most wicked nations of the time. Not only did they worship idols, but child sacrifice (should we read abortion) was part of their ritual. God spoke to Joshua (Joshua was praying) and gave him the strangest, most absurd military strategy ever.

> March around the city once with all the armed men. Do this for six days. Have seven priests carry trumpets of rams' horns in front of the ark. On the seventh day, march around the city seven times, with the priests blowing the trumpets. When you hear them sound a long blast on the trumpets, have the whole army give a loud shout; then the wall of the city will collapse and the army will go up, everyone straight in.[5]

This was the first test for Joshua, and he passed. Now the hard part. There was very little risk for Joshua militarily to lay siege to a city and march around it. Perhaps his pride would be wounded, and he could risk losing credibility, but since the people knew he was being obedient to God, they trusted him. He had earned their trust not through fear but through faithfulness to God.

5. Josh 6:3–5 NIV.

The next one would be to trust God for his provision. These people were marching through the desert. Joshua was tasked with feeding them, and yes, the LORD had provided them with quail and manna, but one could easily see the sacking of Jericho as God giving them permission to take their wealth. It was expected. Joshua told them to devote the city and all that was in it to the Lord, but all its wealth was to be "devoted to the Lord"[6] too. They were given strict instructions to not take any of the wealth unless they want to be cursed. Every living thing including potential food sources were destroyed. It ends with Joshua cursing the city and leaving it behind. It would have been tempting for Joshua to stop here, but he remained faithful and obedient to God and as a result we are told his name spread "throughout the land."[7] The difference between a follower and a fan is obedience. Can you imagine the trust required for Joshua to obey God's seeming illogical instructions? If we know the full outcome of the task God is calling us to complete, there is not a tremendous amount of faith or trust involved. God had not communicated exactly how the entire process would unfold to Joshua, but he was obedient anyway. Regardless of how little sense it made to Joshua, he did exactly as God asked. Are you seeing the pattern yet?

The Jesus Model

We have one more stop in the Old Testament and then we will join Jesus. When we think about prophets' prayer life, we would be remiss to not look at the life of Elijah. This man prayed and it did not rain for three and a half years! Elijah's life is an exemplary life of faithfulness and obedience to God. He was fed by ravens, he witnessed the miracle of provision for the widow whose flour and oil never ran out, he resurrected her son, and stood toe to toe with the prophets of Baal on Mount Carmel and prevailed for YHWH. He even outran Ahab's chariots! That was a fifteen-mile sprint that

---

6. Josh 6:17 NIV.
7. Josh 6:27 NIV.

was only possible because God gave him special "power."[8] All of this was possible because Elijah was not seeking to make a name for himself, but for God. Did you spot the secret sauce Elijah used?

We saved our best example for last: Jesus! At every important milestone of Jesus life, we see him praying to the Father. In fact, before and after anything Jesus does, he is in prayer. In Mark 1:12 we're told the Spirit drives Jesus to the wilderness to pray before he starts his ministry. In Luke 11:1 the disciples find Jesus praying and are so impressed they ask him to teach them to pray. In Matt 14:22–23 after Jesus sends the disciples to the other side of the sea of Galilee, he goes away to pray. Also, in Matt 14:13 he is alone with the Father praying and grieving over the death of John the Baptist when the crowds find him. He prays over a kid's sack lunch and feeds over 5,000 people! But perhaps the most significant time we see Jesus praying to the Father is the garden of Gethsemane which we find in Matt 26:36–46. Jesus is praying so hard and so long here, the disciples fall asleep not once but, three times for which he scolds them. "So, could you not watch with me one hour? Watch and pray that you may not enter temptation. The spirit indeed is willing, but the flesh is weak."[9]

Perhaps this is Jesus most human moment? He knows what is ahead and he confesses that he must pray. He prays so hard his sweat became like drops of blood. We know how it ends. Judas betrays Jesus, Peter denies him, and Jesus is crucified. His last words were prayers. "Father, forgive them for they do not know what they are doing!"[10] He forgives a thief hanging on a cross beside him, and finally, around the sixth hour, he utters his final prayer: "Father, INTO YOUR HANDS I ENTRUST MY SPIRIT."[11]

Prayer = faithfulness + obedience + trust

These are the three ingredients to God's secret sauce. Only then can we be empowered by God to do his will. Joshua did not march and then pray. Elijah did not first challenge the prophets of

8. 1 Kgs 18:46 NIV.

9. Matt 26:40–41 NLT.

10. Luke 23:34 NIV.

11. Luke 23:46 NASB.

Baal before he prayed, neither did it stop rain for over three years before he prayed. Jesus did not climb a mountain of death and hang on a cross to rescued humanity from sin and death before he prayed! Whatever our mission, whatever God's vision for your church, whatever God's will for your life, we cannot do it before we pray.

Everything hinges upon this. I am ashamed to tell you I tried. One of the things I tell the people I coach and mentor and my children is "Listen to me, not because I'm smart, but because I have made a lot of mistakes and I can tell you just as much what *not* to do is I can what to do!" But thanks be to God, he has delivered me from this body of death, and he can and will deliver your church and your congregation too. Just apply that secret sauce! Keep in mind that it is through prayer that God reveals to us what success looks like. Be careful to not look to your denomination, organization, or anyone but God for your definition of success. Resentment is built on the foundation of disappointment and disappointment is fed by poor expectations. In the end God has not called us to success but to faithfulness, faithfulness not to a cause but to him and his ways. Often what looks like death and failure to us is simply a waypoint on the way to resurrection.

8

Establishing Systems to Succeed

Systems are a part of everything. Governments have systems, corporations have systems. Families, the weather, planets, even the human body is supported by underlying healthy systems. Our churches are also reliant upon healthy systems for support. From the outside looking in, it is tempting to look at individual leaders to gauge the healthiness of an organization. It is tempting to study strategies and concepts, personality types, income, location, or any number of factors. Those are all important factors, but all those factors are connected and or related to systems. Systems will literally determine whether our churches or any other organism or organization lives or dies, thrives or barely survives, wilts and withers on the vine or whether it sprouts and springs upward to become a massive oak. Systems are the guts of the planting and revitalization efforts.

In this chapter we'll explore these interdependent systems. We will identify them, their function, and their importance in the overall health and even success of the church. We've discussed the importance of prayer, leadership, and resilience. We've mentioned adaptability, and even the fact that there is not a single approach or solution that guarantees success. However, focusing on the health of these eight systems—in-reach, reproduction, assimilation, worship, spiritual maturity, shepherding care, generosity, and ministry placement—combined with strong, healthy leaders and a robust prayer life, will position you and your team in an environment that is poised for thriving.

Everything Will Not Go as Planned

We know pandemics happen and overnight churches across the nation will close on Easter Sunday, shuttering people around the world in their homes. Additionally, organizations like organisms are living and changing. The church has systems, but so do families. We do not discuss family systems in this chapter except to say that family systems' dynamics will necessarily interact with the leaders as well as the churches and the intermingling of these systems will create stress and unknown dynamics on the healthiest of systems. These and other environmental factors can cause the healthiest of systems to fall into sickness or disrepair. This is where the elements of leadership development and prayer become crucial practices. With these cautions stated, we will begin to digest the guts of the church to help us reflect the glory of God.

In-Reach System

In the infancy of your new church, almost everything rises and falls on the leadership of the pastor. This is also true for revitalization efforts. An existing church in need of revitalization may have a key leader who has significant influence or even a church boss who has an unhealthy influence. It suffices to say that if any revitalization effort is going to be successful, it must be made clear that Jesus is Lord and therefore the boss. The role of the pastor is to discern the Lord's will and carry it out. One reason revitalization is so difficult is that the reason the church needs revitalization is that these systems have become unhealthy. An unhealthy leader, some may call them a church boss, can stand in the way of these revitalization efforts, which is why establishing that Jesus is the Lord of church planting and revitalization is important to any planting or revitalization effort. In its infancy the church is its most vulnerable.

As the church matures the responsibility of leading will necessarily expand beyond the pastor to include others. This is the point at which vision casting, honing the message, and a clear mission become vitally important. Let's call this an elevator speech. As you cast your vision continue to mine it for meaning. Continue to whittle it down into an image that creates interest and curiosity like a casual conversation you'd have with someone on an elevator ride. The point here is not to vomit your vision on the passenger(s), but it is designed to end with an invitation for them to learn more. This is the beginning stages of formulating your in-reach system.

Who's on Your Team?

What is in-reach? In-reach simply means you are reaching into the community instead of focusing inward on your church. The *in-reach system* is crucial to forming your launch team. One of the temptations for the church planter in the infancy stages of planting is to do everything his/herself. Church planters tend to be unicorns. They are rare and unique because they possess so many talents. They are visionaries, but often are people who have a reputation for getting things done. They also often have decent administrative skills, possess energetic personalities, and are intrinsically motivated. Ironically these gifts can work against the planter because they can create a false sense of confidence and self-dependence. Even if the planter or pastor has the gifts to do it all him/herself in the beginning, different sizes of churches require different types of leaders. If a planter cannot learn to delegate and recruit, he/she will plateau or will need to prepare for the eventuality of succession of leadership when the church reaches fifty to seventy people.

The in-reach system is the system that must be developed not only to recruit the launch team, those who will work hand in hand with the pastor to launch the church, but those will eventually be the everyday people from all walks of life: the moms and dads, the awkward teen from down the road who desperately needs a mentor, the tattoo artist, the local pub owner, the landlord, the lady of ill repute, and everyone else. The heart of any planting or revitalization of effort is the in-reach system. Over the last couple of decades much research has been on the reasons for the church's decline in attendance and membership. Simultaneously, they studied the reasons people attended the church. Dr. Marvin Jones examined many factors in his doctoral thesis. He looked at the music style, preaching style, theology, atmosphere, presence of tongues/no tongues, conservative/liberal alignment, attractional element, missional focus, and other factors. Out of everything he studied in the end, the most significant factor for whether someone would attend the church was an invitation—especially an invitation from a trusted friend.[1] If the in-reach system is unhealthy, the planter is unlikely to ever be able to gather the critical mass needed to launch. If the planter has a vivacious personality, he/she may do most of the inviting. Again, this is a mistake, because he/she is likely attracting people to himself and while it may succeed short-term, if this pastor were to ever leave many of those would not remain, leaving the pastor who follows facing a mass exodus. Be intentional about training and equipping others to invite.

Building Better

When building the in-reach system, it might be tempting to fish in other pastors' ponds. In other words, start recruiting from other churches in the area. A recent article from the Christian post headline was emblazoned like a scarlet letter: "Only 3 percent of Christian missionaries worldwide focus on 'unreached' people groups."[2] The purpose of building a church is not to gather a crowd to hear you preach. News flash, regardless of what your mother may tell you, you are not that good! The purpose of a church plant is not even to gather a crowd. If you have this misconception, please quit now. You will not last. In the little bit of time you do last,

1. Jones, *Relevance of Corporate Worship.*
2. Giatti, "Only 3% of Christian Missionaries."

you will become a testimony for another person who has a church wound. Planters who fish in other pastors' ponds are looking for easy catches.

On any given Sunday there are those who are unhappy with the current state of affairs within their church or pastor. It may be tempting to look for these pouting prophets or sad saints. The attraction of these types is they already know how to do church. They know about tithing; they already know about discipleship; they usually already have some leadership capabilities and may even be a current leader in their church. This approach will set you up for failure. You are filling your church with unhappy Christians, and it will not take long for them to become unhappy with you. They will come with their own agendas, whatever that may be, even if they do not recognize or admit it. It may take a month, it may take a year, but they will eventually become unhappy and when they do and they leave, they will most likely take others with them. Hands off other pastors' people. Find your own fishing hole, and shame on other pastors who fish in your pond. Know that God sees them, and they will reap what they sow.

Reaching the Community

Prepare in-reach events within the community. Remember if this a church plant, you most likely will not have a building, and even if you do it is likely to be shared with a school or another church. This is a good thing as it builds a "go and tell" mentality into the DNA of the church instead of a "come and see" mindset. Even if you have an existing church and are revitalizing, I do not encourage you to make the church the center of your in-reach activities. It will help make the shift to an outward focus for your congregation if you do in-reach events away from the church. It will teach them that they are the church, not the building. Pointing back to Dr. Jones' research, before people are ever interested in "coming to see" what you have to offer, they want to know who the people are. If they like the people, they are more likely to come and see the church.

Jesus met a woman at the well in John 4. Jesus was treated with suspicion at first by the Samaritan woman. He was Jew and she was Samaritan. There was no love lost between Jews and Samaritans. Only after Jesus had humbled himself and asked for her help in getting a drink of water was she open to conversation. It did not take long for her to realize Jesus was different. The result was she went throughout the countryside telling others to "come and see." Prior to the pandemic trust in institutions was low. Trust in the church was especially low due to scandals from televangelists to megachurches, the Catholic Church, and even the small local church. The Christian reputation was in tatters. Post-pandemic trust in every institution from government to education is also practically destroyed. People do not trust anyone. The in-reach system is as much about building trust as it is inviting people to come and see. If we invite people to come and see through a marketing campaign or a mailer, they are not likely to be interested. For many, a blind invitation to the local church is an assault. It's like asking a victim to come and visit his/her abuser. It is tempting to think this a recent problem, but before modern-day church abuse, the Pharisees and Sadducees were abusing; before them, kings. There were tribes, factions, and, well, all the way back in Genesis, a sibling rivalry ended in the first recorded murder.

Jesus Holds the Power

Humans do not handle power well, which is why we always point people back to Jesus and he becomes the standard bearer for how we wield power. We do not! We take up our cross. We humble ourselves at the well. We heal the sick, help the lame walk, and provide sight to the blind. The heart of the in-reach system is the heart of Jesus. It is not mass marketing, it is organic. We must train and teach our people that as they go about their everyday lives, they should be intentional about letting the light of Jesus shine. According to the 1918 Archbishop's Committee in the Church of England, "To evangelize is to present Christ Jesus in the power of the Holy Spirit, that men shall come to put their trust in God through Him, to accept Him as their Savior and serve Him as their King in the fellowship of His Church."[3]

The Four Goals of the In-Reach System Are

1. Build relationships with pre-believers.

2. Lead pre-believers to Christ.

3. Nurture new believers in their first steps of faith.

4. Enfold new believers into the church.

Multiplication System

For many, the reproductive system is the last system on their list if it is on their list at all. However, it is the key system to maintaining health. God created us and everything in the earth to reproduce. Elephants have elephants, giraffes have giraffes, and even cells multiply. Before Jesus ever entered the scene multiplication was built into the systems of the Jewish culture. By twelve or thirteen most boys would be paired with someone within the community to learn a trade. They would be mentored by this other person who was skilled in a trade and would become an apprentice. Rabbis would choose from students who had shown a passion for the Torah and perhaps greater skill from secondary schools called the beti (HA) midrash ("house of learning"). Some would really stand out and show extraordinary ability. They would move on to what was called a "talmid." That is the word we translate as "disciple." But we use that word much more casually than the ancient Jewish community. This word stresses the relationship between rabbi (teacher or master) and disciple (student). A talmid of Jesus' day would give up his entire life to be with his teacher. So in Matt 28:10 when Jesus tells the disciples to go and make disciples, this was

3. Mills, "What Is Evangelism?," para. 1.

not a new idea.[4] He was essentially commissioning them as rabbis to reproduce the teachings he had already begin, and indeed had been modeling for the entirety of their time together.

By the time we reach Acts we see the reproductive system of the kingdom on full display. The apostles went from town to town preaching the gospel and planting churches. That was how the apostles acted and we must do the same. After Pentecost, "Day after day they met in the temple area continuing with one mind, and breaking bread in various private homes. They were eating their meals together with joy and generous hearts, praising God continually, and having favor with all the people. And the Lord kept adding to their number daily those who were being saved."[5]

The reproductive system encompasses the plan for discipleship and for planting more churches. There are churches in existence that are fifty-plus years of age and have never intentionally planted a church. They may have had splits or unplanned pregnancies, but those are not healthy. God's design and plan for healthy churches, disciples, and everything in the earth is to reproduce. If your church is not reproducing and if you do not plan to reproduce you are not healthy. You are building a tower of Babel to make a name for yourself, instead of building God's kingdom to reveal the full glory of God. Saint Irenaeus said, "The Glory of God is man fully alive."[6]

Why Do Churches Not Multiply?

Ignorance

It is a sad testament to modern Christianity that many churches think they exist simply to grow bigger. They have no idea Jesus intended for them to reproduce.

4. Acts 2:46–47.

5. Acts 2:46–47.

6. D'Ambrosio, "Man Fully Alive," para. 1.

They Do Not Know How

The good news is if you are planting you know how. But if you find yourself in need of training, Dynamic Church Planting International (DCPI) offers church plant training absolutely free. There are no strings attached. No hidden fees. It is not a sales funnel to get you into their system only to offer you "better" course for an additional cost. You can go online to https://dotacademy. org/ and sign up for an account. They will even assign you a free coach to journey with you through the teaching. They have the How (Church Planting Essentials), the Why (Churches Planting Churches), and six other trainings tracks that are all free.

They Are Afraid

They do not want to lose members. They are afraid the other church might "take" some of their people.

They Think They Do Not Have Enough Money

There are many ways to support a church plant. Money is only one way. But if you believe what you preach about giving on Sunday mornings, you know God loves a cheerful giver.

> Truly I say to you, there is no one who has left house or brothers or sisters or mother or father or children or farms, for My sake and for the gospel's sake, but that he will receive a hundred times as much now in the present age, houses and brothers and sisters and mothers and children and farms, along with persecutions; and in the age to come, eternal life. (Mark 10:29–30)

They Have Been There and Done That

Perhaps they tried planting and failed. Failure is a possibility, especially if you do not plan well. You need the right leader, and a good plan. But I would challenge you to consider your definition of failure. How are you measuring success? Did you reach anyone when you tried the first time? Finally, do you always give up the first time you fail at something? Chances are you know how to walk. How many times did you fall when you were learning to walk? We've all had that sermon that looked good on paper, and sounded good in our heads, but when we preached it, it jut did not go as intended. But we got right back in the pulpit the next time and preached another sermon. So, what if you failed. Learn something from your failure.

They Have No Leader

Every church I have planted God has sent me leaders whom he called to pastor and plant churches. I am confident that if you pray, God will send you a leader. The reproductive system was designed by God at the dawn of creation and therefore is his design for the church as well. The church and his disciples should always be "expecting." A good reproductive system will help prevent unplanned pregnancies.

The Assimilation System

"Resistance is futile!" If you are a Star Trek fan you recognize that sentence as being from the Borg, the archnemesis of Captain Picard, who himself was once "assimilated" by them. The Borg were a collective of alien species that roamed throughout the galaxy assimilating other species and making them part of the collective. They were a difficult and powerful enemy because they worked as a collective. They had a hive mind that was able to communicate across great distances to coordinate and plan. They used the strengths of every species and learned and assimilated all their knowledge. Perhaps a hostile alien species that flies around ripping the limbs off people and replacing their eyes with laser beams is not an ideal metaphor for bringing people into the kingdom of

God, but it is at least helpful inasmuch as it illustrates what happens when all systems work together to make the whole better. The church does this through the assimilation system. The assimilation system is simply the process by which you help people get connected to the church. If this system is not healthy, your church may have fantastic leaders, powerful preaching, and be a virtual Six Flags billboard for Jesus, but you'll never be a church. You will only be an amusement park. People will show up, consume your goods, and leave. If you want a strong heathy church, you will need to design a comprehensive system for turning new people into fully functioning members of the body of Christ.

One of the keys to a strong, healthy assimilation system is biblical hospitality. Perhaps hospitality is one of the most biblical practices of the church. Biblical hospitality is welcoming the stranger. I encourage you to plumb the depths of the topic of biblical hospitality. I could write an entire other book on biblical hospitality. Develop a strong theology of hospitality and spend a great amount of time teaching it to your people. Make it a regular sermon series because people tend to get protective. They see ministry as "my" ministry, "my" seat, "my" position of the board, "my" Sunday School class. And if you are the planting pastor it can even become "my" church. Everyone should be training someone to replace themselves, including the pastor. That is part of the reproductive system. But this is an example of how the systems are interdependent. A good assimilation system will keep the reproductive system fresh.

The Goal of the Assimilation System

The goal is to develop fully devoted followers of Jesus who are integrated into the body of Christ. The body of Christ is one of the churchy terms we use that simply means we want them to be fully engaged with the church. We want them to take ownership of its ministry, and see it as an extension of their families, but with an open-door policy to always be willing to add another seat at the banquet table. We want them to be connected Jesus. Develop a plan that includes procedures for what happens the moment a guest drives onto your property the first time, to the follow-up system that engages them after they leave. At DCPI we use the following rules for when someone visits your church. We believe you should have a process whereby you:

- Demonstrate to first-time guests that you want them to become second-time guests.

- Demonstrate to second-time guests that you want them to become third-time guests.

- Demonstrate to third-time guests that you want them to become regular attenders.

- Demonstrate to regular attenders that you want them to become fully functioning members.[7]

A Few Questions to Ask Yourself
When Developing This System

- What will be your process for identifying and encouraging people who are ready to take the next step?

- How will people find opportunities to be a part of the ministry of the church?

- How will people get connected to other people in the church?

- How will you identify someone who has moved to or finds themselves on the fringes of the church desperately wanting to be a part but are afraid?

- Always evaluate this system for unseen and unintentional barriers.

- Are there ways other than being part of the church, perhaps a mission project, or a community in-reach event, or a partnership with another nonprofit in the area where people may

7. See Wolfe, *Principles of Dynamic Church Planting*.

help you? It is not uncommon for the first contact with a potential new person in your church to be on a mission trip or a community project. Have a plan for getting these people connected to the church.[8]

You do not have to recreate the wheel. There are thousands of ideas for assimilation systems. Find one and tweak it for your context. Be sure to get permission and give credit to the organization from which you borrow the plan. Have you ever met a pastor who would not willingly share his/her ministry strategies and the big ones (like Willow Creek) write extensively about theirs in books? The important thing is to sit down with your leadership team and create a flow chart for every potential touch point when a guest arrives and determine who or which team will be responsible for engaging them each step. If you are unsure invite outside eyes to come and give you feedback. Jeff has developed a resource for additional ideas at https://missionalleadershipcoaching.com/, where you will find mini Kindle books on each system available for download there and other helpful information to learn from and lead your people through.

The Worship System

One of the weak spots of many church plants and in the established church is the worship. When I launched my first church, I'll confess this was my weakest area and it hurt me. I had to lead worship and preach. I used video tracks. They were high quality, and I was a music major in my undergrad. My wife plays the piano/keyboard. Even without videos we could do it. But we did not do it as well as someone whose only role was to lead worship. A quality worship experience is a must and that requires prayerful planning and preparation. A quality worship experience communicates that your church is fresh and alive!

8. See Wolfe, *Principles of Dynamic Church Planting*.

Consider When Building Your Worship System

- Make sure your music is suitable for your context. If your context is younger, then be sure the music is what they are accustomed to hearing. Do not refight the worship wars. If your context is more accustomed to hymns, sing hymns.

- Be sure whoever leads your music is both careful and prayerful. A good worship leader will attract good musicians, but make sure they can work as a part of a team and spend time in rehearsal. Rehearsals are a bonding time for your worship team but are also important for quality worship.

- Will they coordinate music with the message? I know pastors who have entire teams present when planning their messages. They want the worship pastor present, and all staff to get perspectives on the Scripture. The music is then planned around the sermon.

- How will the service end? Does the pastor have a specific song? What is the cue for the worship team to return to close out the service?[9]

Winning Worship

Lighting and sound are important elements of the worship system as well. I suggest investing in a quality sound system. If it needs to be portable, your local music store can help you design a system that is mobile. Lighting can be expensive and can help create a good atmosphere, but never underestimate the power of the Holy Spirit. As a church plant you are most likely not going to have professional lighting.

9. See Wolfe, *Principles of Dynamic Church Planting*.

Be Sure Your Worship Service Has
Good Organization and Flow

Be sure everyone can hear. Be sure it is not too loud. One of my pet peeves in worship is for the music to be so loud people can't hear the voices. Yes, the lyrics may be on the screen, but If I wanted to only hear myself sing, I would stay home and sing in the shower. Be sure there is a proper balance of voices and music. Plan the elements of your service, such as offering, liturgies, baptisms, etc. Long-range planning, planning worship two weeks to three months in advance is very helpful but not always possible. Perhaps this would be a goal to which the worship team aspires as they get more comfortable.

Prepared Sermons

The sermon is as much a part of the worship system as the music and a carefully prepared and planned sermon communicated to the worship team is a necessity for things to run smoothly. A poorly planned worship service will distract from a quality biblical message. I call this noise. Noise is anything that distracts from the work of the Holy Spirit in the service. It might be misspelled words on a slide, it might be a full meltdown of the sound system, or even an angry church member that corners you right before you walk onto the platform. We cannot plan for every inevitability, but a careful plan will inevitably prevent a lot of noise.

Evaluate the Service

Many pastors prefer to do this on Sundays immediately following the service, or return after lunch to confer with the teams. The goal of these sessions is to constantly be improving. To improve we must evaluate the elements that went well and those elements that did not go as well as we had hoped. Did we miss anything? Did the song selection work? Was there anything about the sermon that was unclear? You can devise your own evaluation strategy, but a good evaluation after each service will reap many rewards over time.

The Spiritual Formation System

I said it once already—the church does not exist to give you a platform to gather people on Sunday to hear you preach. We plant churches to make Christlike disciples. We revitalize churches to make Christlike disciples. Planting a church without having a spiritual growth system in place is like plowing a garden without planting seeds. Revitalizing an established church is hard ground that only God can help cultivate. To use a biblical illustration, it's like building your house on sand instead of rock (Matt 7:24–27). Discipleship is a partnership between us and God. God does the work, but we must practice the disciplines.

Eight Steps to Spiritual Formation

STEP 1. Biblically based messages

STEP 2. Consistent theological perspective

STEP 3. Simple steps forward (aspect setbacks, but push through)

STEP 4. Progressive (each lesson requires the participant to take another step)

STEP 5. Complete a spiritual gifts inventories to know your giftings

STEP 6. Complete a personality profile such as the Myers Briggs, or the Essential Enneagram

STEP 7. Introduction to spiritual practices/disciplines such as prayer, meditation on the word, journaling, etc. (self-feeding)

STEP 8. End with an invitation to serve and become more involved within the life of the church.[10]

Consider that you have about two hours a week with your people. If you make them dependent upon you for their spiritual formation

---

10. See Wolfe, *Principles of Dynamic Church Planting*.

and nourishment, they will starve. Imagine feeding a baby for two hours once per week. Yet, many churches do exactly that. They never develop a spiritual growth system that progressively moves people into being fully devoted followers of Jesus and Christ like disciples. Your people will be formed by something. If you do not have a spiritual growth system, that something will not be Jesus. If it's not Jesus you will not plant a church, you will just have a club.

9

The Shepherd System

Too often we complicate things for ourselves. Pastors are typically empathetic personalities that care deeply about people. I have already discussed the importance of self-care. A good shepherding system is as important to creating a healthy dynamic church as the other seven. When it comes to shepherding, I cannot think of a better model than Jesus. He had the perfect balance of self-care and caring for others. He selected twelve disciples to whom he would pour out his life, and three who he would personally mentor. If you do not think carefully about your shepherding system in the beginning, you will find yourself burning the candle at both ends and will eventually run out of candle. When a pastor reaches this point the temptation is to look for shortcuts and falling into ethical or moral failure will become almost unbearable. It is also when the temptation to give up on your church plant or revitalization efforts will be the greatest.

The reality is one person can only offer quality care for about twelve people. Twelve people is a good strong number. You can accomplish a tremendous amount with this size group, and it provides the framework for scalability. Pick twelve strong leaders to surround yourself with and three from this group to mentor. Be intentional about pouring everything you have into these three people. One note of caution. Cross-gender mentorships can provide too much opportunity for inappropriate relationships to develop and boundaries to be crossed. If you are a man, choose men to mentor. If you are a woman, choose women to mentor.

In Genesis Israel, formerly Jacob, had twelve sons. This became the foundation of the church (people of God) that God would use to fulfill his promise to Abraham to make him a great nation and bless all people of the earth through him. Israel has children and wives and by chapter 46 they are an extended family of seventy. By the time they reach the point of the Exodus Moses is overwhelmed with caring for the needs of the people. Moses was busy day and night settling disputes. Jethro sees this and tells him he's headed in the wrong direction. Moses explains he is trying to instruct the people in the ways of God. Moses was essentially doing what he had been since he fled Egypt, shepherding, and he was doing it all himself. It was not just seventy people at this point it was the entirety of Israel's family of traipsing through the desert on their way to the promised land, and Moses decided he was going to handle everything himself. Jethro tells him:

This is too much for you to do alone. Now let me give you some good advice, and God will be with you. It is right for you to represent the people before God and bring their disputes to him. You should teach them God's commands and explain to them how they should live and what they should do. But in addition, you should choose some capable men and appoint them as leaders of the people: leaders of thousands, hundreds, fifties, and tens. They must be God-fearing men who can be trusted and who cannot be bribed. Let them serve as judges for the people on a permanent basis. They can bring all the difficult cases to you, but they themselves can decide all the smaller disputes. That will make it easier for you, as they share your burden. If you do this, as God commands, you will not wear yourself out, and all these people can go home with their disputes settled.[1]

Moses fell into the same trap many pastors fall into. They develop a messiah complex thinking it is up to them to save

1. Exod 18:13–37.

everyone. This is a recipe for remaining small and ineffective. If you are planting a house church, perhaps you will be the only one shepherding, but even in a house church system, if you ever plan to expand beyond a single house, you will have to surround yourself with other leaders who can help shepherd your flock. Plan early in your church plant to set up a strong system of shepherding. Identify leaders in your midst who have the gifts of mercy, shepherding and are empathetic. Develop them as leaders and when the time comes, utilize them to share your load. This will also allow you to leverage the system to utilize multiplication instead of simple addition. The assimilation system is where you identify these gifts.

Multiply this across every aspect of your ministry. Make this a common practice across every system and every position where you develop leaders and mentor others, so you always have leaders waiting in the wings to step up and are sharing the load. It is the only way your church will ever support a bigger size. If you want a fantastic real-world example of this, reach out to Kevin Myers, Dan Reliand, or Jason Berry at 12Stone Church. 12Stone is a multi-site, multi-campus church. They do a phenomenal job of setting up systems for multiplication and shepherding. If they can do it, why not you?

The Ministry Placement System

The ministry placement system is really part of the assimilation system or at least a subsystem. For the purposes of this resource, we divide them, but when you are assessing your context, you may choose to rename or reorganize these systems based on your context. As with everything it is not scientific. Ministry is more art than science, more intuition than fixed rules and procedures. The ministry placement system is exactly what it sounds like. It is placing people in the right position at the right time and season of the church and their lives.

Having the right people in the right place is a key to a church running smoothly. A poorly developed ministry placement system will have leaders in positions for which they are not gifted or for which they do not have a passion. Utilize spiritual gifts assessments, personality profiles, leadership style assessments, etc. These are all tools you can use along with personal interviews and surveys of the people to determine interests to place them in ministry positions where they can thrive. A temptation for us as planters when we have a to-do list that looks like the membership role of heaven is to check things off and get them done. Time is of the essence; we need to move on to the next project. When we do this, we may solve a short-term problem and fill a role short-term, but we create headaches down the road. People become unreliable, bored, or they do not last. Three months or even three weeks down the road you either are forced to have a difficult conversation (dealing with difficult people is another book) and fire a volunteer. Yes! There will be occasions where you must fire a volunteer. However, a good ministry placement system will help reduce the frequency with which this must happen.

I (Jeff) once heard John Maxwell tell the story of when he began his ministry in a small church in Indiana. One Sunday morning a lady approached him before the service to indicate God had laid a song on her heart that he wanted her to sing that morning. Maxwell, being new, figured he couldn't argue with God, so he agreed for her to sing. He says there is not a word in the dictionary to describe how bad she was at singing. When she was done, he was crying, but it was not because the Spirit moved. The next week she returned and told him the same thing. Once more he agreed, and she was just as bad the second time. By the third Sunday he had developed a strategy for handling the situation. When she approached him, he kindly and calmy explained that he was appreciative and that if the Lord moved him during the service to have her sing, he would call her up to the platform. A good ministry placement system will help mitigate those awkward ministry moments.

Serving Like Jesus

Have you ever had luck "advertising" positions in the bulletin or announcing on the screen or even from the pulpit. It seems most people are too shy or assume someone else will do it, even if it has been announced for the last six months. Cast a vision for ministry. Provide a detailed ministry description along with the responsibilities and expectations. Talk about how it benefits the church, God, and his kingdom, but also how it can help fulfill a need in them. You could take a Pollyannaish view of people and say they are all unselfish and eager to help, but the reality is most people do things for a complex set of reasons and most of those folks want to know how helping will benefit them. When you are recruiting, give consideration to how it can meet an unmet need in that person. One example of personal benefit is that high school students are required to have volunteer hours. A rotating stint in the nursery is a good place to earn some of those volunteer hours.

The church is bad about burning people out. Even if someone is gifted for a particular ministry, everyone needs a break. A lack of volunteers can create a sense of "permanence" for a position. When recruiting, set a sunset clause for the position. Perhaps begin with a ninety-day trial period where the church and the volunteer can decide if the volunteer is not a fit for the role with no hard feelings on either side. Beyond the ninety-day period perhaps the position is only for a year. This keeps leadership fresh and mitigates volunteer burnout. It is important that every volunteer has a period where he/she is being ministered to. Therefore, even when someone is in a position for an extended period, be sure to provide breaks during that period where they can attend worship services. If you have multiple services, make sure you have different volunteers for each service.

Develop a Safe Environment

We have heard the horror stories of abuse of children and teens within the church. There is not a denomination or organization that is exempt. The world is full of broken people and sometimes that brokenness causes them to harm others. You need a system in place for child safety training and running background checks. I use MinistrySafe. They have a robust curriculum and can even do the background checks and provide a system for keeping up with those volunteers who have had them. Your denomination or organization may already have a system in place, but *do not* assume just because someone is nice and good with kids that they are a perfect fit. Pedophiles are often a magnet for children.

Utilize technology to check children in and out. If your church has multiple entrances, be sure you have security protocols in place in case of an emergency. Parents are dropping their children off in the care of a stranger. Signage letting the parent know all volunteers have had a background check and that the church has a system of checks and balances to be sure the right child is being returned to the right parent will help those parents feel confident about your children's ministry. You also need to have a system for the teen department. Regardless of the size of your church, these safety protocols must be in place. In the case of planting a church, setting this up before you launch will insure you have the framework for a successful children's and teens ministry. A failure to set this up will come back to cause harm to the ministry and your calling.

Generosity System

Church planters and established church leaders are faith oriented. They are often entrepreneurial types that are accustomed to financial risks. It is true there is some overlap in how a business is run and how a church is run. But one key difference in the generosity system of the church is we are working with donations, nonprofits, and income. The balance sheet of the church is reflective of other people's money. A system of checks and balances and strong accountability must be in place. This includes budgets that are strictly adhered to, and open books that are available for access minus specifics of who gave, but which certainly contain the basics of how much money came in through donations and how it was spent. Your denomination or organization most likely has a policies and procedures manual so I will leave the specifics of this portion to them. But strong stewardship is not optional.

Stewarding the Call

Beyond the specifics of accountability, the purpose of the financial systems is to produce mature financial stewards. Stewardship is seldom about money. If a church is struggling financially, it is usually a sign of another system that is broken. Financial stewardship is a matter of the heart. If one's heart is not fully aligned with God, giving to the church is not likely to be a high priority. The goal of a church plant is to be self-supporting. Since stewardship is a reflection of a person's relationship with the Lord, stewardship could also be considered a subsystem of discipleship. When we are discipling people, stewardship is a foundational principal. However, teaching new believers how to be good stewards of their own income often enables them to be better stewards of the kingdom. Christianity is about helping people thrive now and doing God's will on Earth as it is in heaven as much as it is about one day being united with God in heaven.

The statistics for money problems in the home causing marital stress are widely available. If our peoples' home life is like hell on Earth, it is hard for them to imagine heaven. The first step for them on the path of faithful stewardship might be helping them address "the problem" which has caused the struggle. Once they realize the amount of money they are spending on sin combined with the clarity of mind and the freedom they experience in Jesus, they gladly become faithful tithers.

Dave Ramsey's "Financial Peace University" is a great small group option. There are others out there as well and you may have your own system. The point is to help people take control of their own budgets and often it frees them up to help the church budget. In addition to teaching on money management, be sure you make giving as easy as possible. During the pandemic, churches discovered they had to move to online giving to survive. Depending on the system you use, they will take a portion of the donation in processing fees, so budget for this. Provide many different ministries or projects to which people can give. Often before a person will be a tither, he/she will give to a specific cause such as missions, or a one-time offering for Easter, or a building fund.

God Is in the Details

Do not plan your vision around your budget, plan your budget around your vision. Some people pinch a penny so hard it makes Abraham Lincoln's nose bleed. Sometimes you'll get an accountant type on your stewardship team that is a budget hawk. These people help keep a strong visionary leader from spending into oblivion and can simultaneously be a source of tension. Embrace these people. Make them your friend and work closely with them. As long as they understand your vision and feel heard, they will not stand in your way. Strong visionary pastors must be careful not to bully their church into huge building programs on the promise that they will double or triple the size of the church if only they had a bigger building, only to abandon the programs and the church when things do not go as planned, leaving the congregation with a massive mortgage and unable to do ministry. We need budget hawks.

The Church Needs Systems

You can have grand visions, deep faith, and coffers lined with gold, but if our systems are not functioning or, worse, were never put into place, our churches will never thrive. "I can do all things through Christ who strengthens me."[2] But seldom does God do for us that which we can for ourselves. That is *not* the same as saying God helps those who help themselves. God expects us to have a coherent plan in place. He expects us to train and raise up leaders. Jesus modeled this. He also modeled reproducing and multiplying

2. Phil 4:13 (NASB).

leaders. God is not a God of chaos but of order. Jesus says, "Here I am! I stand at the door and knock. If anyone hears my voice and opens the door, I will come in and eat with that person, and they with me" (Rev 3:20 NIV) Right before this, in verse 19, he says, "Those whom I love I rebuke and discipline. So be earnest and repent." In other words, we have a responsibility to set up the conditions to thrive. Repenting means to turn around and go a different direction. We can gather and pray. We can ask others to pray. We can read our Bibles daily. We can tithe faithfully, and even go and tell others about our new church. However, the reality is that even when they come, our churches will never be what God intended them to be and we will never be able to reach those he intends for us to reach if we do not have the structural systems in place. God desires for us to do what we can and he will do what we cannot do.

10

Creating Healthy Spaces to Plant

EACH SUNDAY PASTORS STAND in the pulpit, looking out over half-empty sanctuaries, and ponder the local church's fate. If one were to wander around the church facilities for long, they would find outdated classrooms with toys that look like they belong in a yard sale, along with old Sunday school literature from years past. All around the church, you can find nameplates with names that many don't remember, and there is a sense that change has not entered the church doors for several decades.

The rubble of the past rises while the established church's hopes and dreams to survive are slowly dying. In the book of Nehemiah, Nehemiah is called to the task of rebuilding the wall. There were many times of disappointment and challenge, yet he never let up on the call on his life. While the facility and grounds look like it's from a past era of Christianity, the church is very much alive. Every day, pastors and lay leaders strive to do their best to rebuild the church using pieces of the past while holding to God's promises in their hearts for the people and community around them. But, to gain a real foothold in the community the church has to become healthy again so she can give birth (plant a church).

In the book of Nehemiah three key components rise to the surface amid the rubble that he faced. It is precisely what pastors and future planters need to remember when they find themselves amid the ruins: *Vision, Connection, and Perseverance.*

Share and Celebrate the Vision

A significant component in a turnaround is all the negative voices that push back against all the change. For far too long, members have gotten used to the church's smell, look, and feel and have forgotten to view the church through guests' eyes. In rebuilding from the rubble, the pastor needs to share God's vision for the church, including preparing for future growth. This part can be painful as people begin to doubt the turnaround, challenge the changes, and try to return to comfortable.

Nehemiah kept sharing each day through conversations with small and large groups the positives of what was taking place while guarding the people against the attacks coming from below. The church revitalizer, too, must protect the people from the pain of others by spreading positive news and stopping the opposing talk from carrying much weight, all while keeping the church focused on moving forward by celebrating victories small and large that are taking place.

Connecting with People and Programs

When Nehemiah arrived to rebuild the wall, he was shocked at the destruction. The once fortified city had seen her walls breached and scarred with black soot from the fire that burned. After assessing the situation, Nehemiah began developing teams of families to step into the breach and start the early task of using current resources to rebuild and obtain new supplies of people and material to reconstruct the breach.

Like Nehemiah, the pastor has to assess the current state of the church and help the people understand the desperate need that they find themselves in. Develop a list of usable resources within the church to recreate a fresh perspective and remove unwanted clutter to intentionally redesign classroom space for future outside use. Expand community connections with other nonprofits developing a community hub inside the church where citizens know the church is there for them and where possibilities are more important than programs.

Persevere to Attain the Promise

Nehemiah faced major opposition from people, and I imagine it was painful to hear and see. However, while the wall should have taken years to rebuild, it instead was reconstructed in fifty-two days. It is a reminder that when people are working together for a common purpose, God can use the faithfulness of his people to do extraordinary things. When a church begins to rebuild from the past, people will try to slow down or stop altogether the good works that the Lord has called the church to achieve. That is when the pastor and the leadership have to persevere to attain God's promises for the local church.

In the infancy of a turnaround, the devil fights the hardest, as it becomes an easy time to discourage, dissuade, or even dismiss a turnaround. The leadership, to be successful, must maintain a prayerful and positive posture that encourages the people to keep pressing forward even when things look bleak. Nehemiah had each worker carry their sword at the ready as they worked, and it's a reminder to the church needing revitalization that a praying people can defeat back the forces of evil for God's good.

It is easy to become discouraged when a leader looks from the pulpit and sees fewer and fewer people weekly. However, Nehemiah shows that God is still at work even in the darkest hour of ministry if the local church's leadership will look for God. The reality you might face today is small compared to the dream of planting and expanding God's kingdom. If you are willing to do your part, God is willing to do his, but are you ready to change to reach the community?

God Is Shifting the Church Culture

The church is experiencing a shift that comes along once in a generation. A generational seismic shift is coming to the church culture and the pandemic and political climate has hastened the shift. The old way of doing things is being transformed into a new opportunity to serve and plant the church with a more extraordinary voice. This shift can be scary for some, but for a church revitalizer or a planter this can be an exciting time to serve forward-leaning churches.

This pandemic earthquake has shaken the spiritual formation of how the church has run. The pandemic and its effects have shown the church that if they stay the same, they will surely disappear into oblivion as the culture around the church has changed. The old tactics of opening the doors and the people will come have been left by the wayside as members have not returned. Visitors have become few and far between for many established churches. But, instead of seeing this as a negative, some leaders and churches are taking this opportunity to advance up the spiritual field to change the church's culture in a positive way to reach more people.

God Shift 1: Evaluate Effectiveness

For far too long, churches have relied on programs to power the church. The programs began to falter when program workers were no longer showing up to help lead them. As the programs became dormant because of a lack of leadership or attendance, the church has evaluated each program's gospel effectiveness. Programs that used to drive the church have driven many into the ground because they no longer are effective or reach their attended audience. The resources (people and financial) have dwindled, but the programs remained. As the aftershock of the pandemic has taken hold, a shift is taking place to eliminate programs that have outlived their usefulness and move much-needed resources to programs that are reaching the lost or training up a new crop of gospel leaders.

God Shift 2: Evaluate Need

As people and finances have dwindled, the system could not sustain past programs and positions. Churches that are rebounding have evaluated the needs around them. The years 2020 and 2021 were measured in lockdowns, mask mandates, and rules that have upset the traditional way of serving the sheep of the church. This God shift has enabled a culture shift to prioritize people over programs. The community's needs around the church campus are seen with a people-focused mentality. As the needs of the people outside the walls are elevated, the conditions inside the walls decrease. This shift has created a missional approach that brings the gospel to life in the lives of believers and opens hearts to plant churches and reach new families.

God Shift 3: Evaluate Response

For decades the established church and their leaders placed resources in areas not by greatest need but by the most significant influence. As the yearly budget was being drawn up, the influencers inside the room used their position to place finances in areas they could navigate as their fiefdoms. These fiefdoms guarded their cache of resources to the detriment of the health of the general church. However, with the God shift post-COVID, leadership had had to face the fact that they could no longer maintain fiefdoms, or the church would die. This realization forced a cultural church shift that made every action evaluable to respond to the church's needs. Narrowing service buckets to a few key areas enabled the church to answer to their neighbors with more resources. No longer was it the case that dollars flowed to the same programs each year, but they were transferred to areas of greatest need.

As the church settles from the God aftershocks of the pandemic, it has a creative opportunity to become the church God wants them to be in this new decade. No longer does the church have to divide ministry into planting or revitalizing the established church. The church can do both, if the local church is healthy and has accepted the God vision to reach new people for Jesus through planting.

About the Authors

DR. DESMOND BARRETT is the lead pastor at Summit Church of the Nazarene in Ashland, Kentucky, where he is married to his wife Julie and has four children. He is the author of ***Revitalizing the Declining Church: From Death's Door to Community Growth*** (2021), and ***Addition through Subtraction: Revitalizing the Established Church*** (2022). He is a host of the podcast ***Revitalizing the Declining Church with Dr. Desmond Barrett***, has done extensive research in the area of church revitalization and serves as church revitalizer, consultant, coach, and mentor to revitalizing pastors and churches.

He is a graduate of Nazarene Bible College (bachelor of ministry), and Trevecca Nazarene University (master of organizational leadership, and doctor of education in leadership and professional practice).

DR. JEFFERY D. SKINNER is currently the global director of Coached DOT Academy for Dynamic Church Planting International, and is a senior master trainer, also with DCPI. He resides near Atlanta, GA, with his wife of thirty years, and has two adopted children: Blaine, who attends Trevecca Nazarene University, and Hayden, who is a sophomore in high school. He is a contributing author to the book ***Uncontrolling Love: Essays Exploring the Love of God***, with an introduction by Thomas Jay Oord, is president of missional leadership coaching and church planting, hosts a weekly podcast entitled ***Echoes Through Eternity***. He has over fifteen years' experience in church planting and over twenty years of experience as an entrepreneur in the IT industry. Additionally, he has done extensive research on reclaiming the salient Christian spiritual identity of the next generations.

He has an undergraduate degree in music and business and a doctor of education in leadership and professional practice from Trevecca Nazarene University, and a master of arts in spiritual formation from Northwest Nazarene University.

Bibliography

Baptist Press Staff. "Study Suggests New View of Church Plants." *Baptist Press*, November 14, 2017. https://www.baptistpress.com/resource-library/news/study-suggests-new-view-of-church-plants/.

Brueggemann, Walter. "The Liturgy of Abundance—The Generous Steward." https://pdf4pro.com/amp/view/the-liturgy-of-abundance-the-generous-steward-2a360d.html.

Carter, Timothy. "The True Failure Rate of Small Businesses." *Entrepeneur*, January 3, 2021. https://www.entrepreneur.com/starting-a-business/the-true-failure-rate-of-small-businesses/361350.

D'Ambrosio, Marcellino. "Man Fully Alive Is the Glory of God—Irenaeus." *Crossroads Initiative*, June 20, 2021. https://www.crossroadsinitiative.com/media/articles/man-fully-alive-is-the-glory-of-god-st-irenaeus/.

Dungy, Tony, with Nathan Whitaker. *The Mentor Leader: Secrets to Building People and Teams That Win Consistently*. Carol Stream, IL: Tyndale, 2010.

Earls, Aaron. "Small Churches Continue Growing—but in Number, Not Size." https://research.lifeway.com/2021/10/20/small-churches-continue-growing-but-in-number-not-size/.

Giatti, Ian. "Only 3% of Christian Missionaries Focus on 'Unreached' People | World News." *The Christian Post*, July 3, 2022. https://www.christianpost.com/news/only-3-of-christian-missionaries-focus-on-unreached-people.html.

HBO Max. "The Batman | Official Trailer | HBO Max." *YouTube*, April 12, 2022. https://www.youtube.com/watch?v=vc7_mH2PWHs.

Hirsch, Alan. "Alan Hirsch: Sparks and Seeds." *Vimeo*, September 2, 2010. https://vimeo.com/14637661.

Bibliography

Jones, Marvin. *The Relevance of Corporate Worship for Generation X and the Millennial Generation.* Nashville, TN: Trevecca Nazarene University, 2015.

Lawlor, Leonard. "Jacques Derrida." *Stanford Encyclopedia of Philosophy.* https://plato.stanford.edu/entries/derrida/.

Maxwell, John. "5 Lessons I Learned When Just Starting Out—John Maxwell." *John Maxwell* (blog), April 26, 2016. https://www.johnmaxwell.com/blog/5-lessons-i-learned-when-just-starting-out/.

Mills, Joshua. "What Is Evangelism?" *Servants of Grace* (blog), November 22, 2021. https://servantsofgrace.org/what-is-evangelism/.

Myers, Kevin, and John C. Maxwell. *Home Run: Learn God's Game Plan for Life and Leadership.* New York: FaithWords, 2014.

Saint John of the Cross. *The Collected Works of St. John of the Cross.* Translated by Kieran Kavanaugh and Otilio Rodriguez. Washington, DC: ICS, 1991.

Tverberg, Lois. "Covered in the Dust of Your Rabbi: An Urban Legend?—Our Rabbi Jesus." *Our Rabbi Jesus* (blog), January 27, 2012. https://ourrabbijesus.com/covered-in-the-dust-of-your-rabbi-an-urban-legend/.

Wolfe, Aaron. *Principles of Dynamic Church Planting.* 3rd ed. Dynamic Church Planting International, 2020. E-book.

www.ingramcontent.com/pod-product-compliance
Lightning Source LLC
Chambersburg PA
CBHW070738030726
47601CB00001B/62